Essential Education
Learning Made CERTAIN

Essential Skills Series Sampler

This sampler provides representative lessons from the *Essential Math Skills, Essential Reading Skills*, and *Essential Writing and Language Skills* workbooks. The sample lessons include one lower level foundational lesson and one higher level lesson from each workbook.

Senior Consultants
Bonnie Goonen
Susan Pittman-Shetler

Published by Essential Education

Essential Skills Series Sampler

ISBN 978-1-940532-10-3

Copyright © 2015 by Essential Education. All rights reserved.
No part of this book may be reproduced in any form or by any means, electronic or mechanical, without written permission from Essential Education, except in the case of brief quotations embodied in critical articles and reviews.

For more information, contact:
Essential Education Corporation
895 NW Grant Avenue
Corvallis, OR 97330
Phone: 800-931-8069

Cover Design: Karen Guard

GED® is a registered trademark of the American Council on Education (ACE) and administered exclusively by GED Testing Service LLC under license. This material is not endorsed or approved by ACE or GED Testing Service.

TASC—Test Assessing Secondary Completion is a trademark of McGraw-Hill School Education Holdings, LLC. McGraw-Hill Education is not affiliated with The After-School Corporation, which is known as TASC. The After-School Corporation has no affiliation with the Test Assessing Secondary Completion ("TASC test") offered by McGraw-Hill Education, and has not authorized, sponsored or otherwise approved of any of McGraw-Hill Education's products and services, including TASC test.

ETS, the ETS logo and HiSET are registered trademarks of Educational Testing Service (ETS) and used in the United States under license. This material is not endorsed or approved by ETS.

Essential Education provides innovative, effective HSE test preparation and adult learning programs centered on the learner's needs.
For more information, please visit http://www.passGED.com/educators/.

Table of Contents

Essential Math Skills

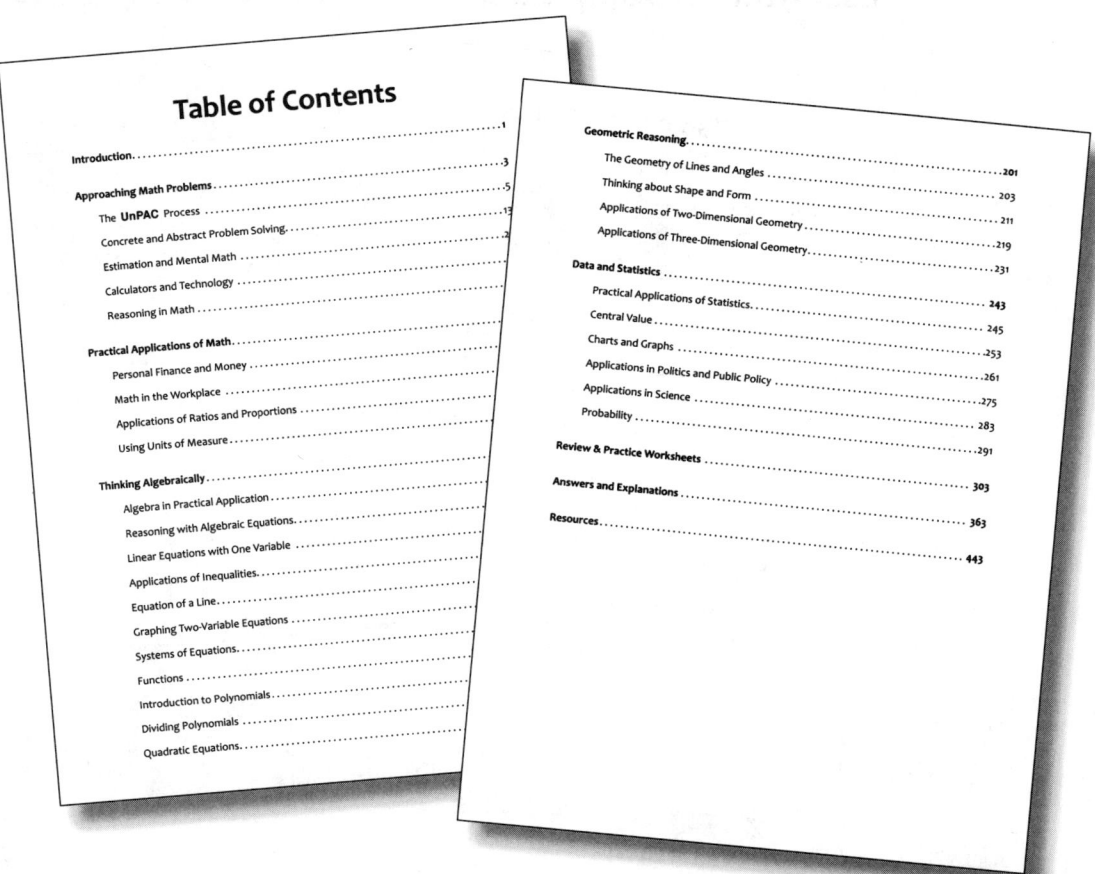

Essential Writing and Language Skills

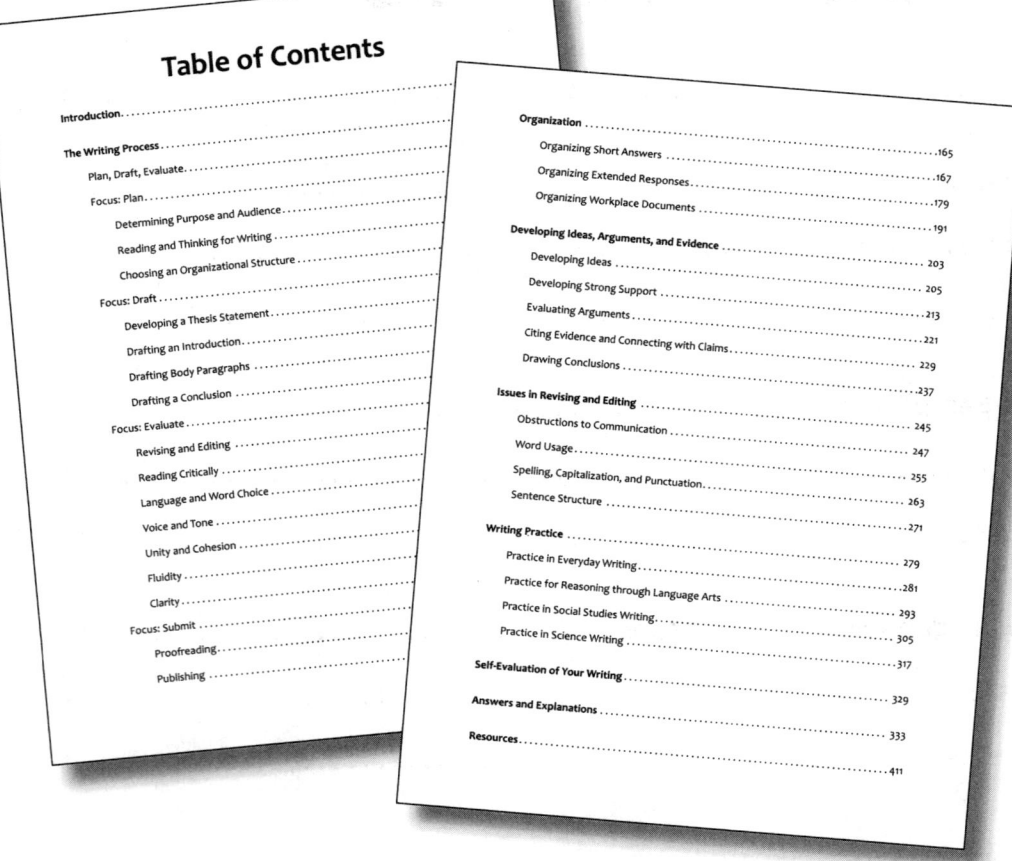

Table of Contents

Essential Reading Skills

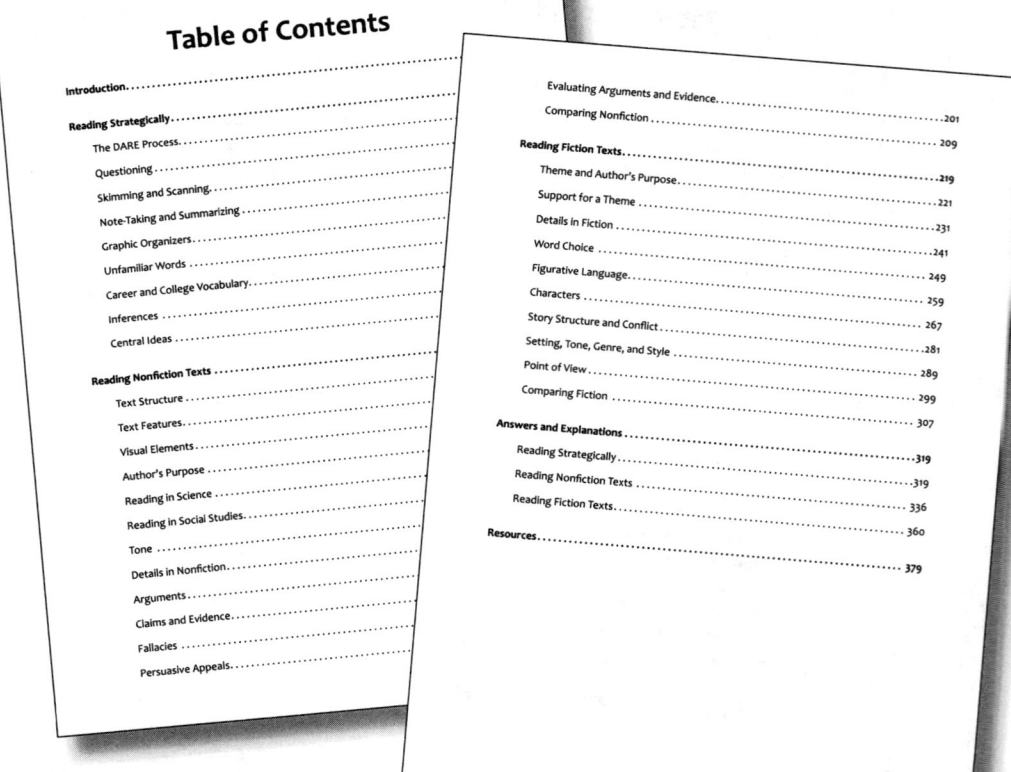

Table of Contents

Introduction

Complete Prep for the GED® Test, HiSET® Exam, and TASC Test

Developed based on the CCR Standards with editorial guidance from Senior Consultants Bonnie Goonen and Susan Pittman-Shetler, the Essential Skills Series workbooks fulfill the growing need for skills-based learning. Each lesson includes a simple strategy for adult students to use to develop a skill. Students apply and expand their knowledge using real-world problems and higher Depth of Knowledge exercises, as well as practicing with questions like those found on the three major HSE exams. Once a student acquires essential skills, those skills can be applied to work, school, and life.

The new high school equivalency tests require a new kind of supplemental text. Skill books and worksheets are just not enough anymore. Students need to demonstrate deep understanding and reasoning skills, and they need to be able to interpret and use complex thinking to solve problems. This is where the Essential Skills series excels and stands alone. Using strategy-based learning, the Essential Skills workbooks prepare people for not only the new HSE tests, but for college and career readiness.

Integrated with GED, TASC Prep, and HiSET Academies

Learning doesn't happen by handing a student a workbook or making her sit through a lecture. Deep learning happens through the integration of multiple learning experiences: reading, listening, interacting, and questioning. Our revolutionary online HSE Academies blend perfectly with the Essential Skills Workbook Series. They reinforce each other in ways that print or online alone cannot do.

Strategic Thinking Included

Rote practice does not give students the basic reasoning and understanding they need to master the new HSE tests. Each lesson in the Essential Skills Series provides a step-by-step approach to understanding. Students' learning is built on strategic skills and modeling of real-life examples.

Connections to Daily Life

Adult Ed students want to know why what they are learning will be useful to them. Each Essential Skills workbook begins with a Connections section that demonstrates how the material can be transferred to the student's daily lives and career pathways.

100% CCSS and CCR Standards

The Essential Skills Series is built on the foundation of CCSS and College and Career Readiness Standards. But standards are not enough to build a curriculum. The Essential Skills Series distills the standards into bite-sized instructional bits for the adult learner.

Essential Education
Learning Made CERTAIN

Essential
Math Skills

Interactive Practice Workbook

Authors

Dianne DeMille

Maya Moore

Teresa Perrin

Brian Seaman

Lara Wheeler

Senior Consultants

Bonnie Goonen

Susan Pittman-Shetler

Published by Essential Education

Problem-solving Strategies to Boost Math Scores

Learn how to solve the math problems on the the GED® test, TASC test, or HiSET® exam quickly and accurately by applying mathematical reasoning skills.

Students learn to connect new concepts to what they already know and then learn strategies to find the answer quickly. The practice questions and thorough answer key show students how to check their work for accuracy and misunderstandings.

Lessons in this book are aligned with Common Core and College and Career Readiness Standards, and cover polynomials, algebra with linear equations, integers, and geometry. Common mathematical problems used in science, social studies, and business are also included.

At 444 pages, this book is a complete test preparation course useful for self-study or to compliment online instruction.

This math book contains practice problems that involve different levels of knowledge and thinking:

- If a problem has one star, it's a procedural problem. You need to apply the right math skills to solve it.

- If a problem has two stars, it will require more thinking through. You'll have to consider options for solving it, and it will show a deeper understanding of math.

- If a problem has three stars, it will really get you thinking about how you approach math problems and about what the math skills you're learning really mean.

Applications of Ratios and Proportions

Connections

Have you ever...

- Needed to convert a measurement from inches to feet?
- Calculated the unit price of something sold by the case?
- Tried to plan the amount of food needed for a party?

Ratios are a useful tool in mathematics because they apply to so many real-world situations. Ratios are all about relationships. Converting measurements, finding percents, and measuring distances on maps can all be done using ratios.

Ratios are fractions that relate one type of thing to something else. For example:

- 12 inches to a foot can be shown as a ratio: $\dfrac{12\ inches}{1\ foot}$
- 25 miles per gallon can be shown as a ratio: $\dfrac{25\ miles}{1\ gallon}$
- Seven pounds of pasta for 55 guests can be shown as a ratio: $\dfrac{7\ pounds}{55\ guests}$

Once you have a ratio, you can divide to find the **unit rate**, the amount per one unit of measurement. For example, if you have driven 225 miles on five gallons of gas in your new hybrid car, you can divide to find a unit rate of 45 miles per gallon.

You can also use ratios to solve **proportions**, which are equations that involve ratios and an unknown. For example, if you know your hybrid car gets 45 miles per gallon, you can calculate the amount of gas for a 398-mile trip with a proportion:

$$\frac{45\ miles}{1\ gallon} = \frac{398\ miles}{x}$$

Learn It!

Solving Problems Using Ratios

A ratio is simply a fraction, but it may have different units in the numerator and denominator.

You will often want to find a unit rate from a ratio. How many miles per gallon did you get on that last road trip? How many stuffed mushrooms will you have for each guest? Miles per gallon, price per pound, and inches per foot are all unit rates. When you write a unit rate as a fraction, the denominator is one.

To find the unit rate if the denominator is not one, divide. If you have seven pounds of pasta for 55 guests, that would be $\frac{7}{55}$, or about 0.13 pounds per guest.

Marie is following a pattern for building a birdhouse, but the measurements are in centimeters and her measuring tape is in inches. She knows that there are 2.54 centimeters in an inch. The roof of the birdhouse should be 25 cm by 30 cm. What are its dimensions in inches?

Write a Ratio

You can write a relationship between two values as a ratio. It is a correct ratio whichever units are in the numerator and the denominator, but to avoid extra steps to solve the problem, put the units that you want in your final answer in the numerator.

? 1. Write a ratio relating centimeters to inches.

When you have a relationship between two things, such as centimeters and inches, you have a ratio. You can write the ratio of 2.54 centimeters to one inch in two ways:

$$\frac{1\ inch}{2.54\ centimeters} \quad \text{or} \quad \frac{2.54\ centimeters}{1\ inch}$$

Since your final answer should be in inches, the first ratio will be easiest. The ratio of centimeters to inches is a **conversion factor**. Since one inch and 2.54 centimeters are equal, the value of the ratio is one. This is true of any fraction where the numerator and the denominator are equal, just as $\frac{4}{4} = 1$. Because the ratio is equal to one, you can multiply any number by this ratio and not change the equivalent value of that number when the units change.

Write and Solve an Equation

Since ratios are fractions, you can cancel common units to help you solve an equation. To get rid of the old units (centimeters in this case) make sure that your conversion factor has centimeters in the denominator. Once you cancel all the units you can, the remaining units should match the units you want in your final answer.

? **2.** Multiply the original measurement by the conversion factor to find the measurements in inches. Round your answer to the nearest tenth.

Multiply both the length and width by the conversion factor.

$$\frac{25\ cm}{1} \times \frac{1\ inch}{2.54\ cm} = \frac{25}{2.54}\ inches = 9.8425\ldots$$

$$\frac{30\ cm}{1} \times \frac{1\ inch}{2.54\ cm} = \frac{30}{2.54}\ inches = 11.8110\ldots$$

Rounded to the nearest tenth, the dimensions are 9.8 inches by 11.8 inches.

Check Your Answer

When doing conversions, it is easy to lose track of the decimal place. Check to make sure that your answer is sensible, and review your math for common errors.

? **3.** Is a birdhouse roof that is about 10 by 10 inches reasonable?

The size of the birdhouse is reasonable. If your answer were 0.98 by 1.18 inches, that would be a hummingbird house! If it were 98 by 118 inches, it would be more appropriate for a family of eagles. The measurements sound reasonable.

Build Your Math Skills

Try solving this problem using the conversion ratio with one inch in the denominator:

$$\frac{2.54\ cm}{1\ inch}$$

What extra steps do you need? Why?

Solve the following problems using ratios.

1. The conversion factor for cups to a quart is $\frac{1\ quart}{4\ cups}$. Manolo is making a party punch that calls for 14.5 cups of limeade, but he only has a quart jar to use to measure the limeade. How many quarts should he use?

   a. Write the ratio or ratios in the best way for this problem. Explain why you wrote the ratios this way.

   b. Find the solution and check your answer.

2. Aikiko is building a wood shed. The blueprint she is using says that one inch on the drawing is equivalent to 1.5 feet. She needs to cut 12 two-by-fours to the right length. In the blueprint, they are five inches long. How long will the two-by-fours be?

   a. Write the ratio or ratios in the best way for this problem. Explain why you wrote the ratios this way.

   b. Find the solution and check your answer.

3. Javier is in chemistry lab. He needs 250 mL of 10% sodium hydroxide, w/v. This means that for every liter of water, he will add 100 grams of sodium hydroxide. How many grams of sodium hydroxide does he need?

   a. Write the ratio or ratios in the best way for this problem. Explain why you wrote the ratios this way.

   b. Find the solution and check your answer.

4. Liz and Deshane work for a painting company. Liz can paint 25 square feet in eight minutes, and Deshane can paint 25 square feet in six minutes. Working together, how much can they paint in four hours?

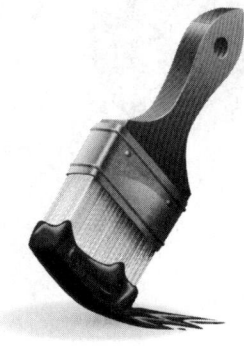

    a. Write two ratios and an equation relating them.

    b. Answer the question and check the answer.

5. Destinee and Sarah are working together on a problem that says: "Convert 743 millimeters to inches using the following information. There are 1000 millimeters in a meter, 100 centimeters in a meter, and 2.54 centimeters in an inch." Sarah showed the following work. She knows it is wrong because it is so large. Inches aren't that much larger than millimeters. How could Destinee correct it for her?

$$743 \ mm \left(\frac{1000 \ mm}{m} \right) \left(\frac{100 \ cm}{m} \right) \left(\frac{in}{2.54 \ cm} \right) = 29,251,968.5$$

    a. Identify the ratio or ratios that are incorrectly used.

    b. Solve the problem. Round to the nearest tenth.

    c. What advice would you give Sarah to avoid this error in the future?

Cross-Multiply and Divide

You can solve any proportion with the cross-multiply and divide strategy. If you have one fraction equal to another fraction, multiplying denominators across the equals sign eliminates fractions. Then, divide to isolate the variable.

Cross-Multiply	Divide

$$\frac{a}{b} \diagdown \frac{c}{x} \quad ax = bc \qquad\qquad \frac{ax}{a} = \frac{bc}{a} \quad x = \frac{bc}{a}$$

$$\frac{2}{3} \diagdown \frac{4}{x} \quad 2x = 3 \times 4 \qquad \frac{2x}{2} = \frac{3 \times 4}{2} \quad x = \frac{3 \times 4}{2}$$

At the grocery store, peaches are priced at five pounds for $3.00. You have $4.50. Assuming there is no tax, how many pounds of peaches could you buy?

Find the Relationship

Find the relationship in the question. Look for the words *per* or *for*. These words usually indicate a relationship that can be written as a ratio. Write the ratio as a fraction, including the units.

?　　1. Identify the given relationship in the problem and write it as a fraction with units.

The given relationship is five pounds for $3.00. You can write this as a ratio:

$$\frac{5 \; pounds}{3 \; dollars}$$

You could also say that three dollars buys you five pounds and write it $\frac{3 \; pounds}{5 \; dollars}$.

The ratio can be written either way, since it is equivalent to one. Three dollars is equivalent to five pounds of peaches at the grocery store, so the ratio is equivalent to one.

Write a Proportion

Using the ratio on one side of the equation, write a proportion. There should be a fraction on the other side of the equation. The other fraction will have the same units, in the same places, and will use another given value (in this case, $4.50). You can use x to represent the unknown. Once you're sure your units line up, you can remove them.

? **2.** Write a proportion to solve the problem.

Review &
Practice

Get extra practice
with the worksheet
for ratios and
proportions on
pages 325–326.

Using the ratio of pounds to dollars, you can write a proportion
to solve the problem:

$$\frac{5\ pounds}{3\ dollars} = \frac{x}{4.5\ dollars}$$

$$\frac{5}{3} = \frac{x}{4.5}$$

Cross-Multiply and Divide

You want to know the value of x, so you want to isolate x on one side of the equation. You
can solve any proportion by first cross-multiplying (multiply the denominator of each fraction across the equal sign) and then dividing by the new coefficient of x.

? **3.** Solve the proportion.

Essential Math Skills includes
a 60-page section of practice
worksheets and review.

Step 1: Cross-multiply.

$$\frac{5}{3} = \frac{x}{4.5} \quad \times \quad 4.5 \times 5 = 3x \qquad 22.5 = 3x$$

Step 2: Divide.

$$\frac{22.5}{3} = \frac{3x}{3} \qquad \frac{22.5}{3} = x$$

You can buy $\frac{22.5}{3}$ or 7½ pounds of peaches.

Check Your Answer

Make sure that the answer is logical and check for errors in your math.

? **4.** If you could buy five pounds for $3.00, does it make sense that you can buy seven and a
half pounds for $4.50? Why?

$4.50 is one and a half times $3.00. It makes sense that you could buy one and a half times
as many peaches for $4.50 as for $3.00. Since one-and-a-half times five pounds is seven and a
half pounds, the answer makes sense.

Practice It!

Write and solve proportions to answer the following questions.

 1. Sophia wants to find the gas mileage of her car. When she fills the tank, the odometer reads 92,481 miles. When she fills it again, the odometer reads 92,692. It takes 9.3 gallons to completely fill the tank. What is the gas mileage of Sophia's car, to the nearest hundredth?

a. Find the relationship and write a proportion.

b. Solve the proportion and check your answer.

c. Identify an error you might make in solving this problem. How could you avoid that error?

2. A new test for Lyme disease is 87% accurate in detecting if someone has the disease. If 12,400 people who have Lyme disease are tested, how many cases will not be detected?

a. Find the relationship and write a proportion.

b. Solve the proportion and check your answer.

c. Identify an error you might make in solving this problem. How could you avoid that error?

3. You are driving across the country from Phoenix to Boston, a distance of 2,648 miles. You make the first 500 miles in seven hours, including stops. If you can keep up this rate, how many more hours will it take you to get to Boston? Round your answer to the nearest tenth.

    a. Find the relationship and write a proportion.

    b. Solve the proportion and check your answer.

    c. Identify an error you might make in solving this problem. How could you avoid that error?

 4. $\dfrac{2.5}{19} = \dfrac{4.9}{x}$

    a. Solve the proportion.

    b. What is a different way that you could solve this proportion? Compare the two methods.

 5. Henderson's Groceries offers three pounds of medium prawns for $8.61, and Grocery Time offers five pounds for $12.50. Which store has the best price for prawns?

    a. Solve the problem.

    b. What is a different way that you could solve this problem? Compare the two methods.

6. John and Hasim are studying together. The problem they are working on says: The sales tax on a $400 stereo is $38. At the same tax rate, how much would the tax be on a $650 stereo? John does the following work. Hasim knows that the tax wouldn't be less on a more expensive item.

$$\frac{400 \ dollars}{650 \ dollars} = \frac{x}{38 \ dollars}$$
$$38(400) = 650x$$
$$x = \frac{38(400)}{650} = \$23.38$$

a. Identify the mistake.

b. Solve the proportion.

c. What advice would you give John to avoid this error in the future?

 7. Carlos and Tam both commute to work. Carlos traveled nine miles through bumper to bumper traffic at 15 miles per hour. Tam lives farther away, 21 miles. His commute as distance d in miles to time t in minutes is represented by the graph. Who arrives at work sooner, and by how much time?

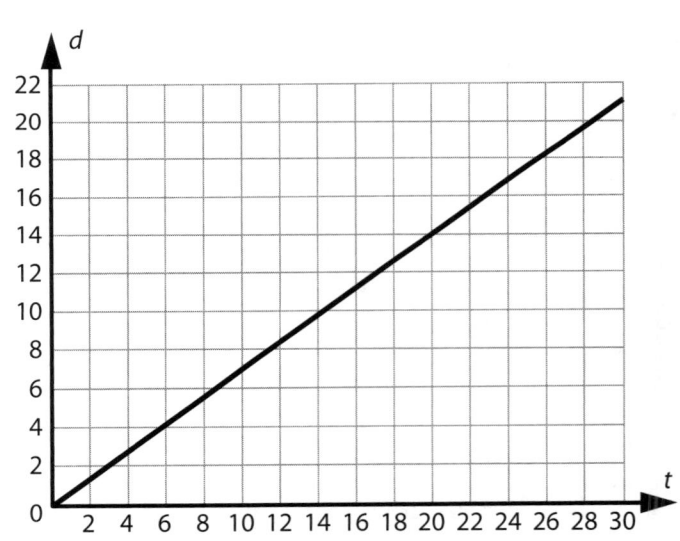

Check **Your Skills**

Answer the following questions using your knowledge of ratios and proportions.

1. If your truck gets 15 miles to the gallon, how many miles can you go on an 18 gallon tank of gas?

    a. 1.2 miles

    b. 270 miles

    c. 27 miles

    d. 2,700 miles

2. You are looking at buying a used car. One car costs $8,100 and gets 22 miles per gallon. Another costs $10,500 and gets 27 miles per gallon. With gas prices averaging $4 per gallon, how many miles would it take for the more expensive car to make up for the difference in cost?

    a. 2,400 miles

    b. 3,000 miles

    c. 600 miles

    d. 1,920 miles

3. Construction has begun on the lot next door to your house. On the blueprint, the building measures 27 cm wide and 15 cm long. The scale of the blueprint is 1 cm = 3 feet. If the lot for this building is 100 feet wide, and the building is centered on the lot, how many feet are there between the building and the side of the lot?

4. A manufacturing company has set a goal of a maximum of two defects per 1,000 capacitors produced. The company ships out 350,828 capacitors. Use the following figures to create an equation showing how many capacitors should be functional for the company to meet its goal.

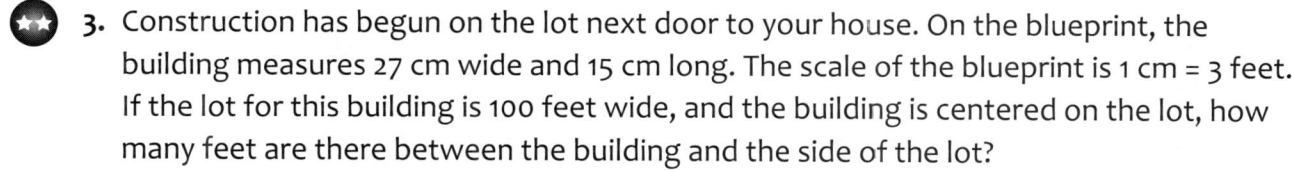

5. The large meteorite that blasted through Russia's sky in February 2013 had an average density of 3.6 g/cm³. Dmitri found a rock that weighed 0.12 pounds and had a volume of 13.21 cm³. The density would need to be within 0.2 g/cm³ of the average for the rock to have been possibly part of the meteorite. How far is the density of the rock from 3.6 g/cm³? Round your answer to the nearest tenth.

> **Math Tip**
>
> Learn common values for conversions.
>
> 1 mile = 1,609 meters
>
> 1 mile = 5,280 feet
>
> 1 pound = 453.6 grams
>
> See page 304 for a table of common units of measure.

6. Grayson and Mo are heading downtown, a distance of 3.5 miles. The bicycle odometer says they are going 24 miles per hour. How many meters per minute are they traveling?

7. Andre's Grocery has a special on mangoes, four for $3.50. Pearson's is advertising mangoes for five for $7.25. How much do you save if you are buying 10 mangoes from the cheaper store?

    a. $4.00

    b. $5.75

    c. $6.50

    d. $7.25

8. An experienced mechanic can change a head gasket in about five hours. Her apprentice would take eight hours to complete the task. If the mechanic works for two hours and then turns the job over to the apprentice, how long does it take the apprentice to complete the job?

9. Jude is on the swim team. He swam the 50-meter breaststroke in 32.74 seconds. What was his speed in miles per hour, rounded to the nearest hundredth?

    a. 0.68 mph

    b. 40.95 mph

    c. 3.42 mph

    d. 12.67 mph

> **Remember the Concept**
>
> Ratios are fractions that show a relationship.
>
> Use a ratio to convert units of measure.
>
> Cross-multiply and divide to solve proportion problems.

Functions

Have you ever...

- Used military time, such as 0800 hours?

- Converted inches to centimeters?

- Determined profit or loss of a business venture or fund-raising activity?

These are all examples of relations. A **relation** is a relationship between two variables that creates ordered pairs (x, y). Any equation with x and y is a relation. A **function** is a special relation that follows an additional rule: For every x, there can be only one y.

A function is like a machine. You put in a value (x), such as five inches, and it gives you a single corresponding value $f(x)$, such as 12.7 centimeters. Functions can be very useful. For example, the time 12:00 can be confusing. The number 12 can point to two values, noon and midnight. However, military time goes from 00 hundred hours to 2400 hours. 1200 hours means noon, not midnight. Military time is a function: one number means exactly one time.

A function can be a set of points, a table, or an equation. The **domain** of a function is the set of input values (x), graphed on the x-axis. The **range** is the set of output values that the function gives you for x, graphed on the y-axis. For every input value (x), there is only one output value, $f(x)$. If you think of ordered pairs as couples, you could say that x is monogamous (although $f(x)$ is not required to be).

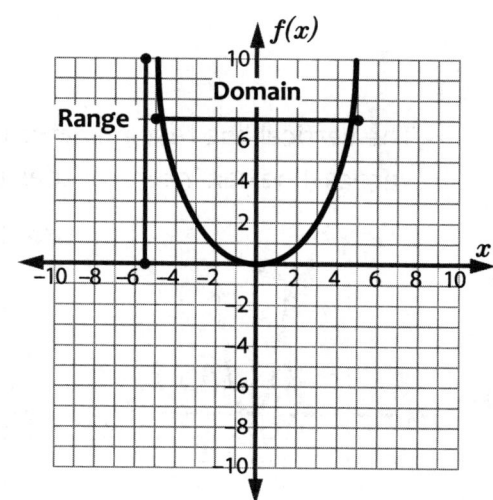

Graphs of straight lines are relatively simple. Functions also include curved lines of many shapes, sometimes graphing complex equations. Even if the equation is complicated, you can understand a lot of information by simply examining the graph of the line.

Understanding Functions

When evaluating a function (finding the $f(x)$ for a value x), keep in mind how functions are written. The notation $f(x)$ means the function of x.

- $f(x)$ is the same as y; it refers to the value associated with a given x.

- $f(1)$ means, "Evaluate the equation (find y) when $x = 1$." What output do you get for this input?

At work, you are examining relationships between profit (x) and several variables. You want to know which variables are a function of x and how profit affects them. When does a certain amount of profit have only one outcome? How does the variable change in the first unit of profit? Determine which graphs are functions. For each function, find $f(0)$ and $f(1)$, and calculate the rate of change between them.

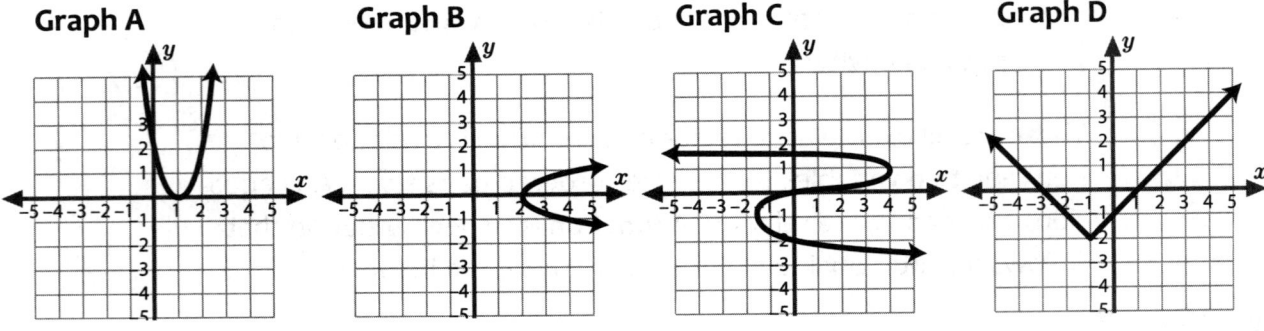

The Vertical Line Test

A graphed relation is a function if you cannot draw a vertical line anywhere on the graph that intersects the graph more than once. This is called the vertical line test.

? 1. Use the vertical line test to determine which graphs show a function.

The vertical line test indicates that graphs A and D are functions. Graphs B and C are not. A vertical line can intersect these graphs at two or more points.

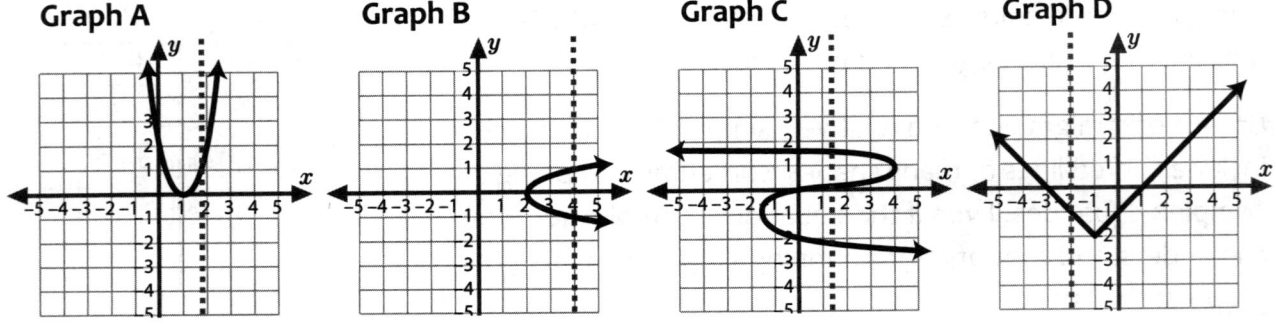

The Value of the Function at a Point

To find $f(x)$ using a graph of a function, simply locate the y value for a specific x. Find the value x on the x-axis. Then follow the grid line up or down until you reach the graphed line. This point is the ordered pair (x, y) which you can think of as $(x, f(x))$.

? **2.** Find $f(1)$ and $f(0)$ on graphs A and D.

Notice that $f(0)$ is the same as the y-intercept, the place the graph intersects the y-axis. For graph A, $f(0)=2$, and for graph D, $f(0)=-1$. Find $x=1$ on the x-axis to locate $f(1)$. For graph A, $f(1)=0$. For graph D, the function of one is the same: $f(1)=0$.

Graph A   **Graph D**

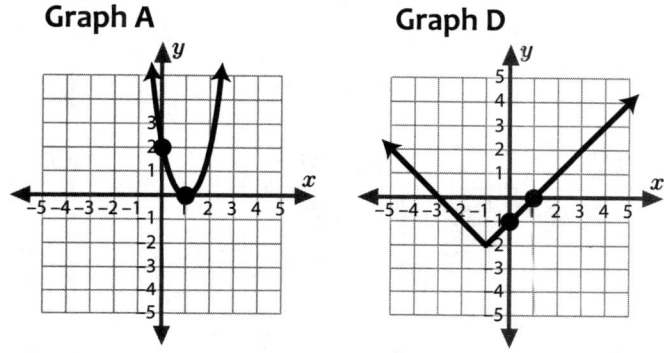

Rise over Run

Even if a function is not a straight line, you can find the average rate of change between two points in the same way you calculate slope. Calculate "Rise over Run" between the points.

? **3.** Find the average rate of change of each function between $x=0$ and $x=1$.

For graph A, the two points are $(0, 2)$ and $(1, 0)$. To find the rate of change, find the slope.

$$\frac{change\ in\ y}{change\ in\ x} = \frac{0-2}{1-0} = -\frac{2}{1} = -2$$

For graph D, the two points are $(0, -1)$ and $(1, 0)$. To find the rate of change, find the slope.

$$\frac{change\ in\ y}{change\ in\ x} = \frac{0-(-1)}{1-0} = \frac{1}{1} = 1$$

The variable in graph A is reduced by the first unit of profit (though it goes up after that). In graph D, the variable increases at a steady rate as profit increases. The graphs allow you to evaluate the relationships between variables.

Use the graphs provided to answer the following questions about functions.

1. Which of these graphs is not a function? Why?

A

B

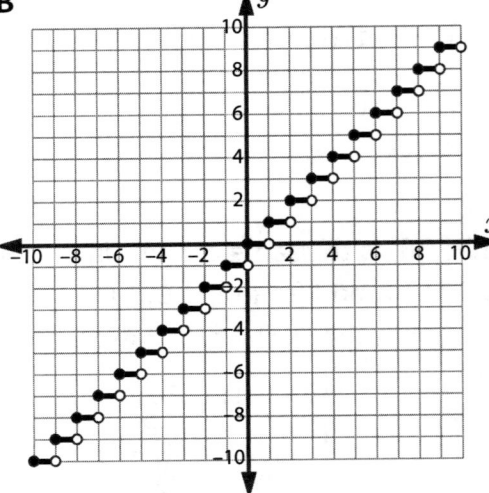

C

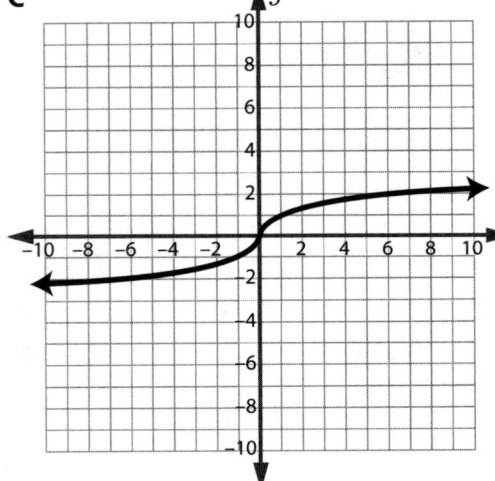

D

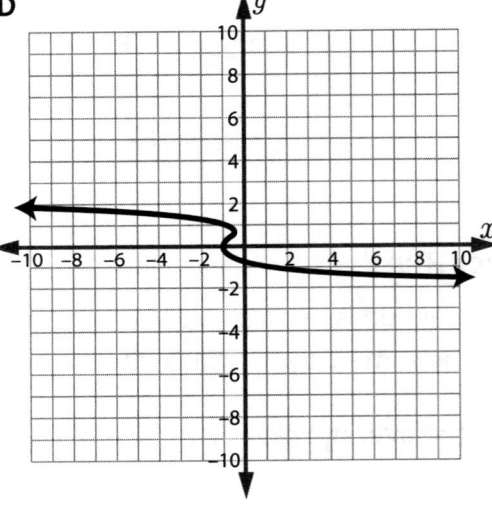

2. $f(x) = -3(x-1)^2 - 4$

a. Find $f(-2)$.

$f(-2) = -3(-2-1)^2 - 4$

b. Find $f(3)$.

c. Find $f(0)$.

3. Consider the function $f(x)$ represented by the table and the function $g(x)$ represented by the graph.

x	y
−1	−3
0	4
1	5

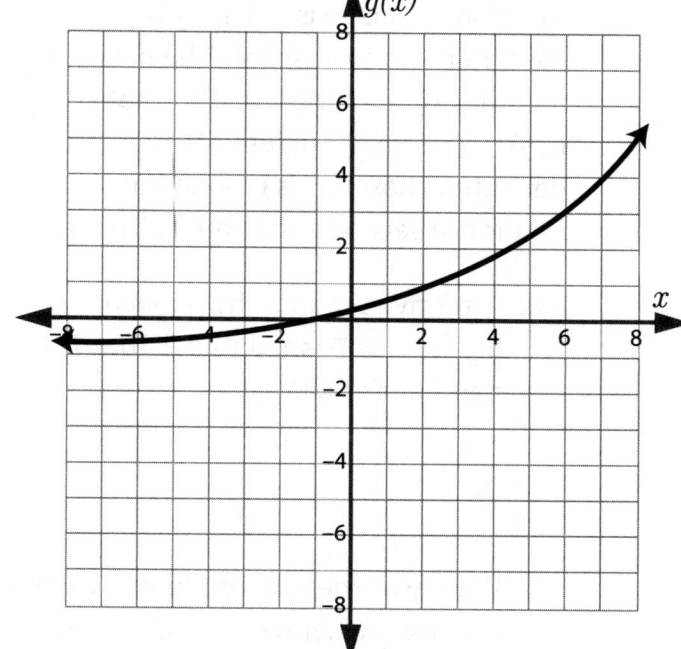

a. Find the average rate of change of each function from −1 to 1.

b. Which function has the greater rate of change from −1 to 1?

 4. Two foam balls are dropped from the side of a bridge 22 feet in the air. The first has a parachute. Its height $f(t)$ in feet at time t in seconds is given in the table. The second has no parachute and falls at a speed indicated by the equation $g(t) = -16t^2 + 22$, where $t = $ time in seconds and $g(t) = $ height in feet.

t	$f(t)$
0	22
0.5	21.5
1	20
1.5	17.5
2	14
3.32	0

a. How much farther has the second ball fallen after one second?

b. To the nearest hundredth of a second, how much time passed between when the first ball and the second ball landed?

5. The height of a baseball after it is hit follows a **parabolic** path (a symmetrical curve) that can be modeled by a function. Dashaun is teaching his daughter to play baseball. The height in feet of Dashaun's baseball is graphed by $f(t)$. The height in feet of his daughter's baseball is graphed by $g(t)$. t = time in seconds after the ball is hit.

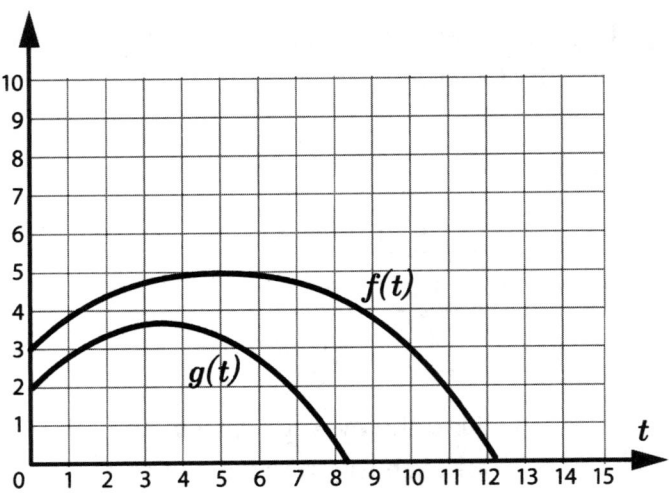

a. After five seconds, how much higher was Dashaun's ball than his daughter's ball?

b. What was the average rate of climb for Dashaun's ball in the first five seconds? In other words, how fast did its height increase in feet per second?

6. Kayla and Jose are working on a physics experiment. Kayla propels a baseball from the ground straight up into the air, and Jose measures its height in feet. Its height as a function of time follows this graph. From the graph, Jose estimates that after three seconds, the ball is about 0.4 feet high.

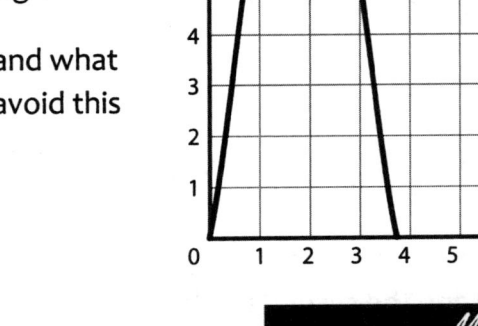

a. What mistake did Jose make, and what advice would you give him to avoid this mistake in the future?

b. How high is the ball after three seconds?

Math Tip

Parabolas are graphs of quadratic functions. Learn more about quadratic equations on page 193.

Describing Graphs of Functions

To understand and compare graphs, you need to be able to describe them. The following terms will help you describe graphs of functions.

Terms Describing Graphs of Functions

Intercepts	Points where the graphed function crosses an axis are **intercepts**. At the x-intercept, y is zero. At the y-intercept, x is zero.
Maximum and Minimum	The highest point on the graph is its **maximum**. The lowest point on the graph is its **minimum**. The **global** maximum or minimum is for the entire graph, and the **relative** maximum or minimum is for a part of the graph.
Positive and Negative	The function is **positive** where y is positive (above the x-axis). It is **negative** where y is negative (below the x-axis). The x-intercepts are called **zeros**, where the value of the function is zero.
Increasing and Decreasing	Where the slope is positive, slanting up to the right, the function is **increasing**. Where the slope is negative, slanting down to the left, the function is **decreasing**.

You are examining a graph of change in a stock price (y) over the days (x) before and after a merger. Find the intercepts, maximums and minimums, the intervals where it is increasing and decreasing, and the intervals where it is positive and negative. What do these features mean?

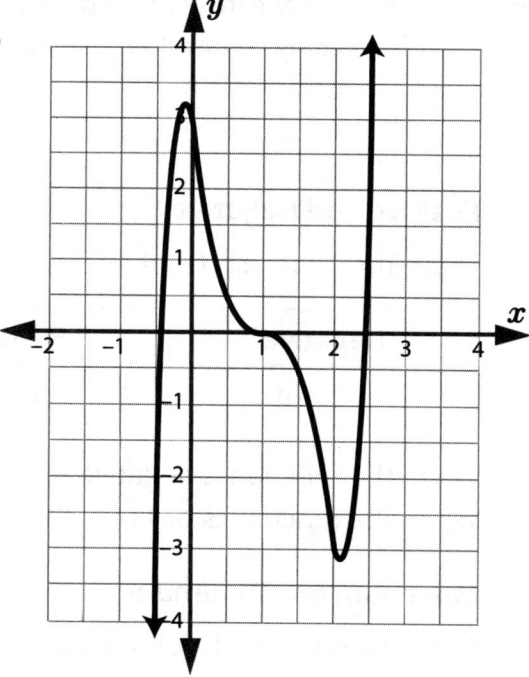

Locate Important Points

Locate the following important points:

- The x-intercepts (zeros) and the y-intercept

- Maximum and minimum points, where the graph reaches a peak or a low point

1. Identify the intercepts, maximums, and minimums. What do these features mean?

On the graph, you can see the approximate locations of the intercepts, maximums, and minimums. You might not know the exact amounts, but you can find an approximate amount.

At the x-intercepts $(0.4, 0)$, $(1, 0)$, and $(2.4, 0)$, y is zero, and the stock price is not changing. At the y-intercept $(0, 3)$, x is zero, so the merger is occurring.

There is a maximum at roughly $(-0.1, 3.2)$, meaning the stock price hit a high in positive change just before the merger. There is a minimum at $(2.1, -3.2)$, meaning that the stock price hit a low in negative change about two days after the merger, before turning upward again. The maximum and minimum are relative, because the graph goes on beyond the graphed area.

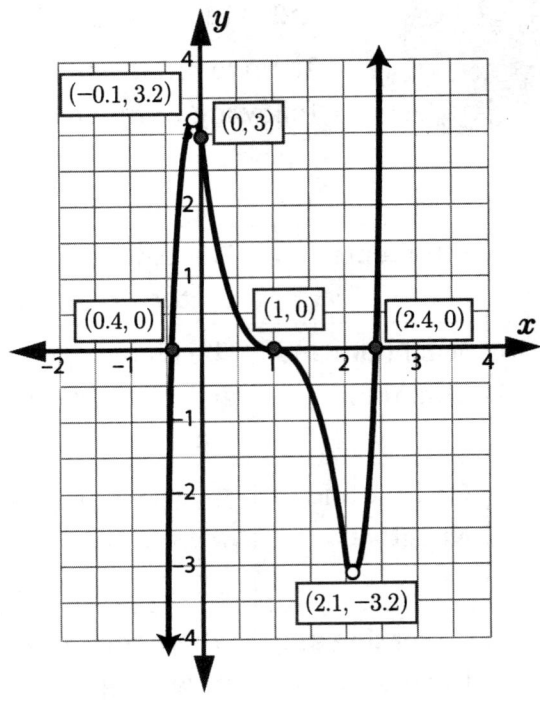

Locate Important Intervals

Use the intercepts to describe where the function is positive and negative. Use the maximums and minimums to describe where the function is increasing and decreasing. Write the results as inequalities using x.

?   **2.** Describe the intervals where the function is positive, negative, increasing, and decreasing. What do these intervals mean?

Positive and Negative

The x-intercepts are $(-0.4, 0)$, $(1, 0)$, and $(2.4, 0)$, so the intervals are:

Negative	Positive	Negative	Positive
$x < -0.4$	$-0.4 < x < 1$	$1 < x < 2.4$	$x > 2.4$

When the function is negative, the stock change is negative, and the stock price is falling. When the function is positive, the stock change is positive, and the price is rising.

Maximum and Minimum

The maximum was $(-0.1, 3.2)$, and the minimum was $(2.1, -3.2)$, so the intervals are:

Increasing	Decreasing	Increasing
$x < -0.1$	$-0.1 < x < 2.1$	$x > 2.1$

There is a little blip at the x-intercept $(1, 0)$, but it actually only decreases slower there. When the function is increasing on $x < -0.1$ and $x > 2.1$, the rate of change of the stock price is increasing, even if the change itself is still negative. When function is decreasing on $-0.1 < x < 2.1$, the rate of change of the stock price is decreasing.

Answer the following questions about graphs of functions.

 1. This graph shows the price of stock ABC over 12 months from January through December.

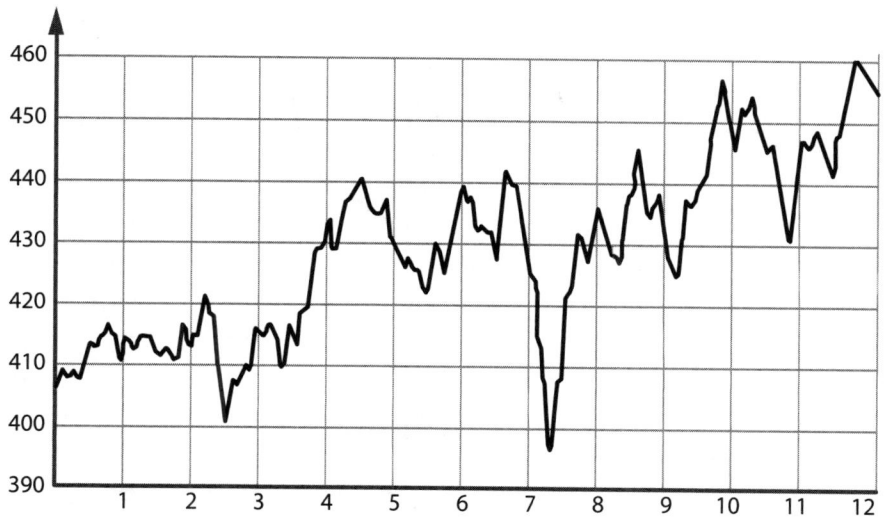

a. What are the maximum and minimum points for this graph?

b. What do the maximum and minimum points represent?

 2. This graph displays the balance in Jon's bank account over a month.

a. What are the x-intercepts, and what do they represent for Jon?

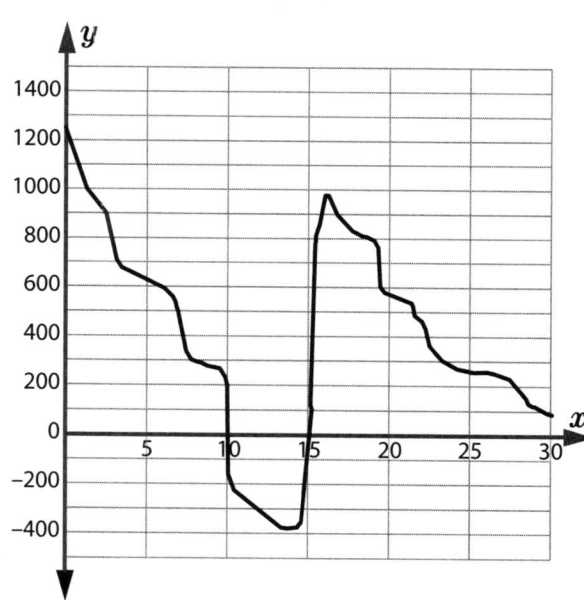

b. Where is the function negative, and what does that represent?

c. Describe what happened on the 10th and on the 15th. Use positive and negative numbers to describe changes in the graph.

3. Frank prepared this graph of his department's productivity in terms of revenue. On what intervals is the graph increasing and decreasing? What do these intervals indicate?

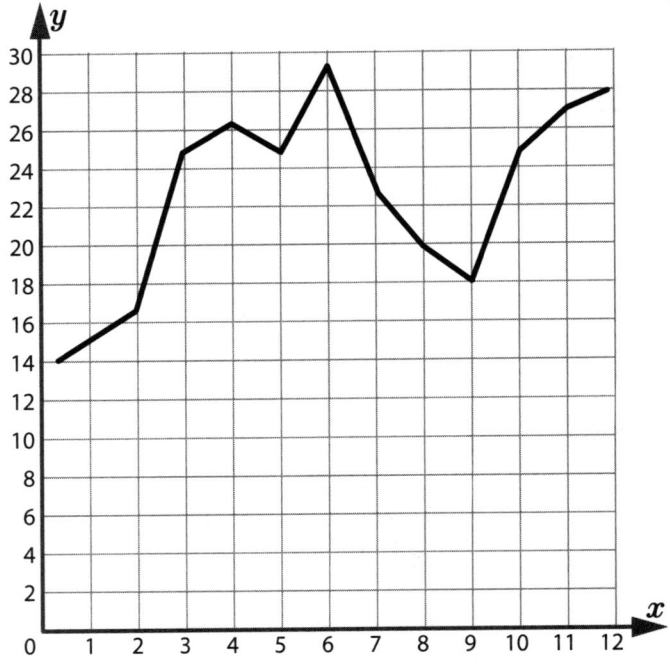

4. This graph represents the function $f(x) = x^2 + 3$. Describe the graph's intercepts, maximums and minimums, the intervals where it is increasing and decreasing, and the intervals where it is positive and negative.

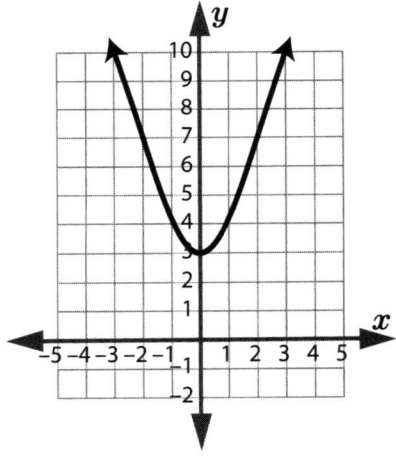

Essential Math Skills includes a 60-page section of practice worksheets and review.

Review & Practice

Get some practice with the quadratic equations on pages 359–360.

Check Your Skills

Answer the following questions using your knowledge of functions.

1. Which of the following does not give y as a function of x?

   a.
   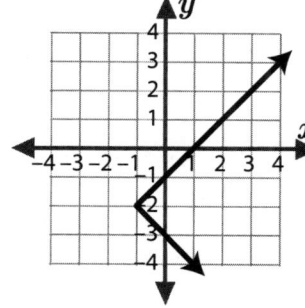

   b.
   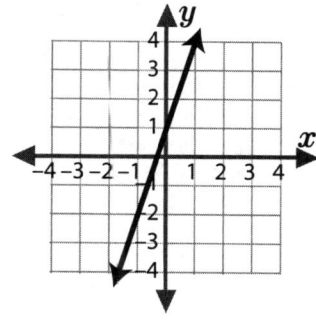

   c. $\{ (0, 1), (2, 3), (4, 5), (5, 4) \}$

   d. $y = 4x^2 + 3$

2. This graph shows the profit p in thousands of dollars based on projected sales of dining room table sets priced at x dollars.

   Mark the point on the graph that indicates how much the company should charge for dining room table sets to maximize profit.

   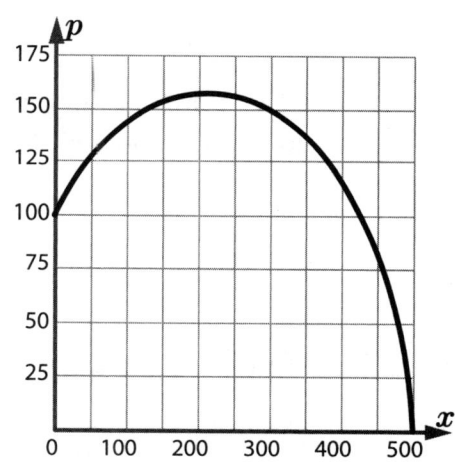

3. Marta presents an advertising campaign to her company that she says will increase sales s, in thousands of dollars, over t years according to the graph. Approximately how much will sales increase in five years?

   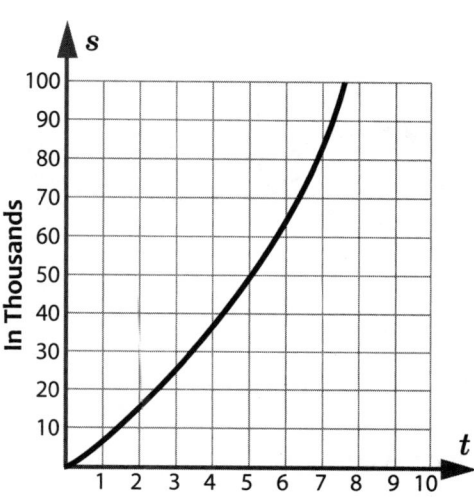

4. Olina and Pilar take an archery class together. Olina has greater strength, but Pilar's shots are more accurate. Olina's arrows tend to follow a trajectory of $f(x) = -0.03(x-14)^2 + 10$, where x is horizontal distance in feet and $f(x)$ is the vertical distance in feet. Pilar's follows the graphed line. After each archer's arrows have travelled 10 feet horizontally, how much higher is Olina's arrow than Pilar's?

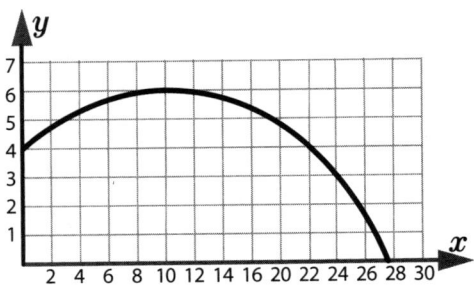

5. For the function $f(x) = 0.01x^2 + x + 4$, find the slope of the line between the graphed points where $x = 10$ and $x = 12$.

6. Where is the function increasing and decreasing?

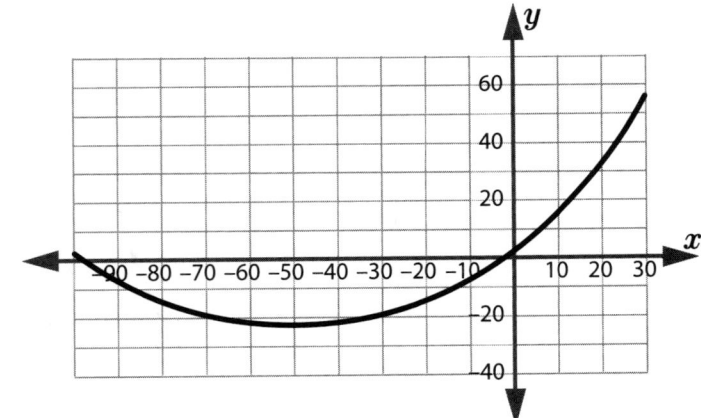

Increasing: $x >$ _____

Decreasing: $x <$ _____

Remember the Concept

In all functions, x has only one y value.

To evaluate $f(a)$ find the value of the function when $x = a$.

The intervals on a graph are defined by the values on the x-axis.

Essential Education
Learning Made CERTAIN

Essential Reading Skills

Interactive Practice Workbook

Authors
Omie Drawhorn

Teresa Perrin

Senior Consultants
Bonnie Goonen

Susan Pittman-Shetler

Published by Essential Education

Boost Test Scores in Reading and Language Arts

This book teaches students to identify and break down the important parts of any text to better comprehend the author's meaning and purpose. Lessons develop the literacy skills necessary to take on college and career-level reading.

Lessons connect new ideas to familiar concepts. Students learn to approach reading tasks efficiently using purpose-driven reading strategies. Practice questions help students test out the strategies and check their work.

Aligned to Common Core and College and Career Readiness Standards, this book focuses on developing vocabulary skills and a knowledge of central themes, arguments, literary conventions, story structure, and point of view. Science and social studies texts are presented along with fiction and nonfiction texts.

Use the 36 complete lessons to support classroom teaching or as a self-study guide. The 380-page book is filled with graphic organizers and helpful visual reminders to improve student's reading comprehension and prepare for the GED® test, TASC test, or HiSET® exam.

This reading book contains practice exercises that require different levels of knowledge and thinking:

★ If an exercise has one star, it's checking if you can follow the procedure you've been learning. You need to apply reading skills, identify elements of a text, or complete part of a clear-cut strategy.

★★ If an exercise has two stars, it will require more thought. You'll have to consider options and show a deeper understanding of reading.

★★★ If an exercise has three stars, it will really get you thinking about how you approach reading and how you think about what you read.

Inferences

Have you ever...

- Decided what gift would be best for a friend?
- Picked a meeting place that your friends would like?
- Formed a first impression about somebody?

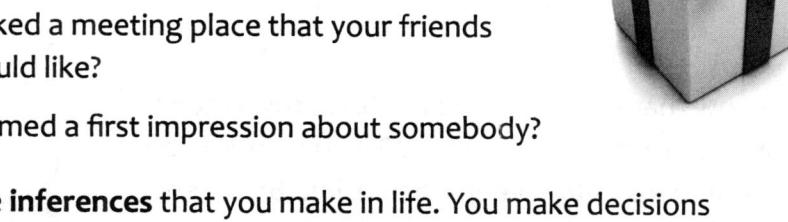

These are **inferences** that you make in life. You make decisions based on what you know about your friends and what you see when you first meet someone. It's a natural reaction to use what you know to make **inferences**.

An **inference** is a conclusion that you make based on information that you have. Every day, you make conclusions that no one told you directly. Reading is the same. You use clues from the text and your own knowledge of the world to make inferences.

- Some information in a text is stated clearly.
- Other information is implied through details in the text.

You use information in the text along with own personal experience to make an inference. Have you heard of "reading between the lines" or "making an educated guess"? That's the same as making an inference.

Inference = What You Know + Clues from the Text

Learn It!

Making Inferences Using an Inference Chart

An inference chart helps you analyze details and your own knowledge to make and understand inferences.

Use this passage for the exercises that follow.

Let's examine the facts. Death row inmates cost the taxpayers millions of dollars each year. It costs far more to prosecute a death penalty case than it does to imprison a convict for life without the possibility of parole. Just maintaining security on death row is incredibly expensive, even without taking into account the cost of countless appeals.

Did you know that U.S. prisoners on death row often wait years before they're executed? The time between sentencing and execution keeps increasing. Between the years 2008 and 2009 it went up by over 20%. In 2010, the average time between sentencing and execution was almost 15 years. Nearly 25% of prisoners on death row die of natural causes, meaning that the state has paid a premium price for a sentence of life in prison.

Choose a Detail

First, choose a significant detail. If you want to understand the author's perspective, find a detail that seems to show the author's feelings or beliefs.

? 1. Select a detail that shows the author's perspective and write it in the chart.

Detail or Clue	What I Already Know	Inference

You might choose the statement: "Death row inmates cost the taxpayers millions of dollars each year."

Review What You Already Know

Identify what you know that can help you make an inference.

? **2.** What do you know that can help you make an inference from the detail in the chart? Add it to the chart.

Detail or Clue	What I Already Know	Inference
"Death row inmates cost the taxpayers millions of dollars each year."		

You might realize that people are often critical of government spending for programs they oppose politically.

Make an Inference

Review details and background knowledge to make an inference.

? **3.** State your inference in the chart.

Detail or Clue	What I Already Know	Inference
"Death row inmates cost the taxpayers millions of dollars each year."	People are often critical of government spending for programs they oppose politically.	

You might conclude that the author is opposed to the death penalty.

? **4.** Add another inference to the chart, using the same passage.

Detail or Clue	What I Already Know	Inference
"Death row inmates cost the taxpayers millions of dollars each year."	People are often critical of government spending for programs they're against politically.	The author is opposed to the death penalty.

Practice It!

Read the passage and answer the questions that follow.

Company Policy on the Use of Technology

Internet Use

Internet use on company time must be for only business-related purposes. As you use the Internet, be careful of the sites you visit. Confidential company information could be compromised. By visiting an insecure site, you could download a virus or spyware that would damage the system and allow people outside the company to access private information.

Company computers are not allowed to view any pornographic, inappropriate, or non-business-related sites. Doing so can lead to action against you, and depending on the case, an end to employment with us.

Email Use

Email should be used for company business only. Do not reveal private company information to people outside the company. Also, remember that non-business related emails (even to coworkers) waste company time. Viewing pornography or sending pornographic jokes or stories via email is considered sexual harassment and will be addressed according to our sexual harassment policy.

Any emails that discriminate against employees based on race, gender, nationality, or religion will be dealt with according to the harassment policy. These emails are not allowed. Sending non-business emails will result in disciplinary action that may lead to an end of employment.

Reading for Understanding

Never lose sight of the text. Base your inferences on the facts. Notice when a conclusion doesn't have support in the reading.

Company Owns Employee Email

Keep in mind that the company owns any email sent through the company email account and any document stored on a company computer. Management has the right to look at any emails or files on your computer at any time. Please do not consider any emails, Internet use, or documents that are created or stored at work to be private.

1. Complete the following inference chart.

Detail or Clue	What I Already Know	Inference
"you could download a virus or spyware that would damage the system and allow people outside the company to access private information"		
"Any emails that discriminate against employees based on race, gender, nationality, or religion will be dealt with according to the harrassment policy."		
"Keep in mind that the company owns any email sent through the company email account and any document stored on a company computer."		

 2. Curtis has been sending personal emails to coworkers on company time. Based on the description of what is acceptable work email and Internet use, what inferences can you make about what will happen to Curtis if he is caught?

3. Becca is applying for a job at a different company and saves her job application on her work computer. What could be the consequences of this? What should Becca do differently, if anything? Explain your reasoning.

4. Which of the following sites can you infer would be appropriate to visit at work? Select all that apply.

   ❑ A website that allows you to download music for free

   ❑ Websites that belong to the company's competitors

   ❑ Google, to perform company research

   ❑ Twitter, to see what your coworkers are posting in their personal accounts

   ❑ Twitter, to see what your company and its competition are posting in their business accounts

5. Dwayne is very anxious about whether his new sneakers have been shipped from the manufacturer yet. What is the company's policy about Dwayne checking the website to see if it has shipped? What details in the text support your answer?

6. Try writing text that causes the reader make an inference. Sarah is really nervous about the test today. Write three to five sentences that give the reader clues about how Sarah feels and why, without actually telling the reader that Sarah is nervous.

Using a Chart to Support Your Inference

When you make an inference, it's important to know what information led you there. It helps you prove you've made a good inference. You can use an inference chart to help define the reasons for an inference.

Susan left in the middle of the film and exited into a dark, empty street. As she looked for a taxi, she noticed the gray-coated man at the bus stop.

Holding her breath, Susan backed up under the cover of the marquee. Had he seen her? She was lucky. He was looking away. Now he turned his face to the theater doorway, and her heart raced as she hid in the shadows.

Susan had nowhere to go but back inside the theater. As soon as he glanced away, she ducked through the glass doors and past the attendant, into the dark, anonymous theater seats. What now?

Make Your Inference

We all make inferences every day. You probably normally infer things about what you're reading, but you might not always be able to clearly state why.

1. How does Susan feel when she sees the man? Write your inference in the chart.

Detail or Clue	What I Already Know	Inference

Though the text doesn't say how Susan feels when she sees the man, you probably infer from her actions that she is afraid.

Identify Supporting Details

Now, find a detail that leads you to believe that Susan is afraid. When a character's feelings aren't explicitly stated, you can infer how she is feeling through descriptions of her actions and words.

2. List one detail that shows you how Susan is feeling.

Detail or Clue	What I Already Know	Inference
		Susan feels afraid.

One supporting detail is that Susan hides when she sees the man.

Connect to What You Already Know

If you've ever been afraid, you can relate to Susan's actions when she sees the man. By thinking about your own experience, you can often relate to what others are experiencing.

3. What do you already know that can help explain Susan's actions? Write it in the chart.

Detail or Clue	What I Already Know	Inference
Susan hides when she sees the man.		Susan feels afraid.

An example of what you know might be that people hide when they're afraid or don't want to be seen.

4. Using the passage, find another supporting detail for an inference.

Detail or Clue	What I Already Know	Inference
Susan hides when she sees the man.	People hide when they're afraid or don't want to be seen.	Susan feels afraid.

Practice It!

This passage is from *The Picture of Dorian Gray* by Oscar Wilde. In this passage, the painter has just finished his portrait of Dorian Gray.

Read the passage and answer the questions that follow.

As the painter looked at the gracious and comely form he had so skillfully mirrored in his art, a smile of pleasure passed across his face, and seemed about to linger there. But he suddenly started up, and closing his eyes, placed his fingers upon the lids, as though he sought to imprison within his brain some curious dream from which he feared he might awake.

"It is your best work, Basil, the best thing you have ever done," said Lord Henry languidly. "You must certainly send it next year to the Grosvenor. The Academy is too large and too vulgar. Whenever I have gone there, there have been either so many people that I have not been able to see the pictures, which was dreadful, or so many pictures that I have not been able to see the people, which was worse. The Grosvenor is really the only place."

"I don't think I shall send it anywhere," he answered, tossing his head back in that odd way that used to make his friends laugh at him at Oxford. "No, I won't send it anywhere."

Lord Henry elevated his eyebrows and looked at him in amazement… "Not send it anywhere? My dear fellow, why? Have you any reason? What odd chaps you painters are! You do anything in the world to gain a reputation. As soon as you have one, you seem to want to throw it away. It is silly of you, for there is only one thing in the world worse than being talked about, and that is not being talked about. A portrait like this would set you far above all the young men in England, and make the old men quite jealous, if old men are ever capable of any emotion."

"I know you will laugh at me," he replied, "but I really can't exhibit it. I have put too much of myself into it."

Lord Henry stretched himself out on the divan and laughed.

"Yes, I knew you would; but it is quite true, all the same."

From *The Picture of Dorian Gray* by Oscar Wilde, 1890

Reading for Understanding

Consider the alternatives. Don't just accept the first inference that comes to mind. Consider details in the text and possible explanations.

1. Use the details from the passage and your background knowledge to finish filling out the chart.

Detail or Clue	What I Already Know	Inference
		Basil likes the painting he's just finished.
		Basil and Lord Henry are friends.
		Basil is a successful artist.

2. Based on the passage, what kind of relationship does Basil have with Lord Henry?

3. What does Lord Henry mean when he says that "there is only one thing in the world worse than being talked about, and that is not being talked about"?

4. How are Basil's feelings about the painting different from Lord Henry's? What details led you to that conclusion?

Check Your Skills

Read the passage and answer the questions that follow.

A recent study has established a connection between autism and attention deficit/hyperactivity disorder (ADHD) in children. Nearly 30 percent of children with autism also show signs of ADHD. That figure is three times higher than it is in the general population.

Doctors say that they don't know what causes ADHD in most cases. That is similar to autism, where the cause is usually unknown. Both disorders affect the brain and its functioning, and something that affects the brain and causes one developmental issue is also likely to cause another developmental issue.

Children in the study with both autism and ADHD had a harder time learning and socializing than children with just autism. Children with autism who aren't seeing improvements in their treatment, where they need to focus on specific skills, may benefit from undergoing ADHD treatments.

Common symptoms of children with ADHD include not being able to wait their turn, interrupting others, fidgeting with items when eating, or not being able to go slower.

Out of 62 children with autism aged four to eight, 18 (29 percent) also showed signs of ADHD.

The director of the Center for Autism Spectrum Disorders called the connection "not surprising." In children who are severely autistic, ADHD can be more of a challenge to identify. However, if parents and teachers notice that attention or activity problems are getting in the way of a child's ability to make progress, they shouldn't hesitate to seek help, the director noted.

 1. Which of the following is the most accurate conclusion based on this study?

    a. A child with autism is more likely to have ADHD than other children.

    b. A child with autism is less likely to have ADHD than other children.

    c. Autism may cause ADHD.

    d. ADHD may cause autism.

2. Based on the text, what are the symptoms of ADHD? Select all that apply.

- ❑ Lack of concentration
- ❑ Fatigue
- ❑ Interrupting
- ❑ Severe shyness
- ❑ Trouble sitting still

3. What is the most likely reason that the director says that the increased occurrence of ADHD in those with autism is "not surprising"?

- **a.** Children with autism are susceptible to many other health concerns.
- **b.** The causes of both disorders are unknown, so the same thing causes both.
- **c.** Earlier studies have shown the same thing.
- **d.** Symptoms of the two conditions resemble each other.

4. Which of the following is the most likely reason that ADHD is harder to spot in children with severe autism?

- **a.** Children with severe autism won't cooperate for the study.
- **b.** Children with autism are better at hiding their ADHD.
- **c.** The symptoms of autism can be similar to those of ADHD.
- **d.** In some cases, children with ADHD won't show symptoms.

5. In undiagnosed cases, which probably is **not** a sign that parents should treat their child with autism for ADHD?

- **a.** They notice their child can't focus in school or social settings.
- **b.** Treatment for autism isn't working.
- **c.** Their child's grades are in trouble.
- **d.** A child is more helpful with chores.

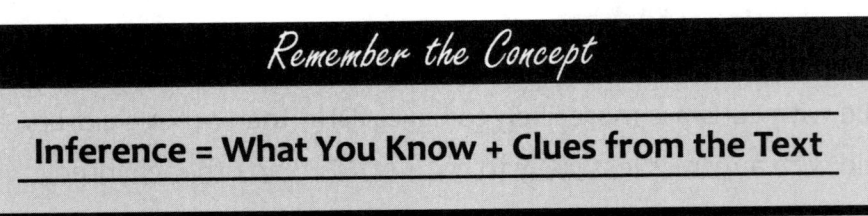

Remember the Concept

Inference = What You Know + Clues from the Text

Claims and Evidence

Have you ever...

- Been unable to decide if you agree with an editorial?

- Had a tough time choosing how to vote on a proposition?

- Found it difficult to believe a product's advertisements?

Every time you make a choice or listen to an opinion, you're evaluating an argument. To evaluate an argument effectively, it helps to identify the **claim**—the author's point—and the **evidence**—how the author supports the claim.

Arguments center around a **claim,** which the author attempts to show is true.

A **claim** is...

- Not a factual statement.

- Argued as either true or false.

- Backed up with **evidence.**

A claim alone is not enough to persuade a reader. If someone makes a claim, you'll likely ask, "Why?" Evidence gives you reasons to help you decide whether an argument is valid. Evidence includes data and examples that connect to and support the claim.

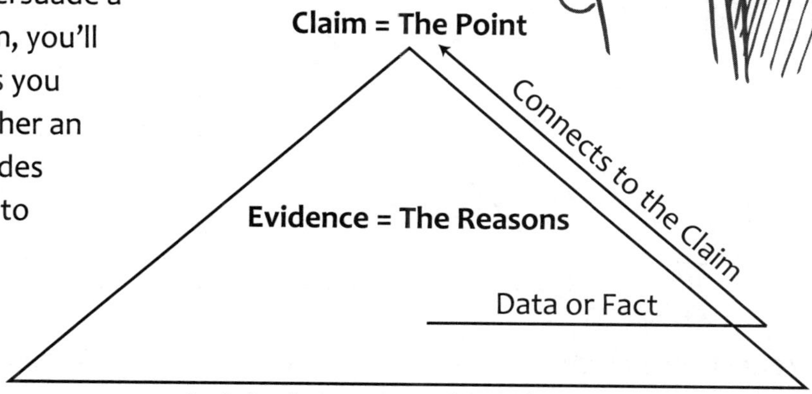

Claim = The Point

Connects to the Claim

Evidence = The Reasons

Data or Fact

A claim is supported by evidence.

The Claims and Evidence Pyramid

Identifying the claim and evidence in an argument helps you to more effectively evaluate the author's stance.

Use this passage for the exercises that follow.

When I was attending college, living off campus was the most freedom I'd ever felt. I spent my freshman and sophomore years living in the dorms. I found the experience cramped, uncomfortable, and miserable. Luckily, I found a quaint but affordable apartment of my own during my junior and senior year. Living off campus gave me the independence and freedom I had craved for so long. I could be myself without worrying about what others thought. I could concentrate on my studies and see people I wanted to see. Having my own kitchen and bathroom provided me with the convenience I needed at a fraction of the cost of living in a dorm. It was a sanctuary I could retreat to when I needed to regroup after a particularly tough day. It also introduced me to life off campus, which is nonexistent while living in the dorms. I was exposed to the life and vibrancy of the larger community.

D *Determine the Purpose*

Imagine you are trying to decide whether to live on or off campus at college. Your sister sent you the above email. Evaluate what she's saying to determine if you agree with her advice.

A *Approach the Text*

To find out what your sister is claiming and why, identify her claim and evidence. A good plan is to skim the text to identify the claim. When you're reading, look for specific evidence.

? **1.** Skim the text and write the claim at the top of the pyramid:

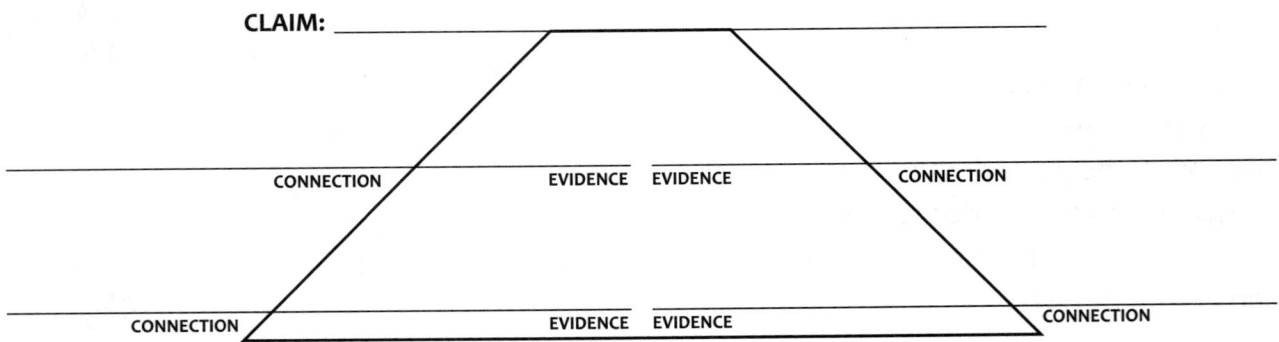

Your sister's claim is that you should live off campus. A claim is often stated toward the beginning of a text. Here, the claim isn't stated directly, but you can infer it by skimming.

R *Read*

As you read, identify the evidence that supports the claim. An effective argument includes evidence that is relevant, sufficient, and credible. Look for:

- Examples
- Reasons
- Facts
- Anecdotes
- Statistics

After you find supporting evidence, look for the link between the evidence and the claim. Why does this evidence help prove the claim?

? **2.** Complete the pyramid with evidence from the passage.

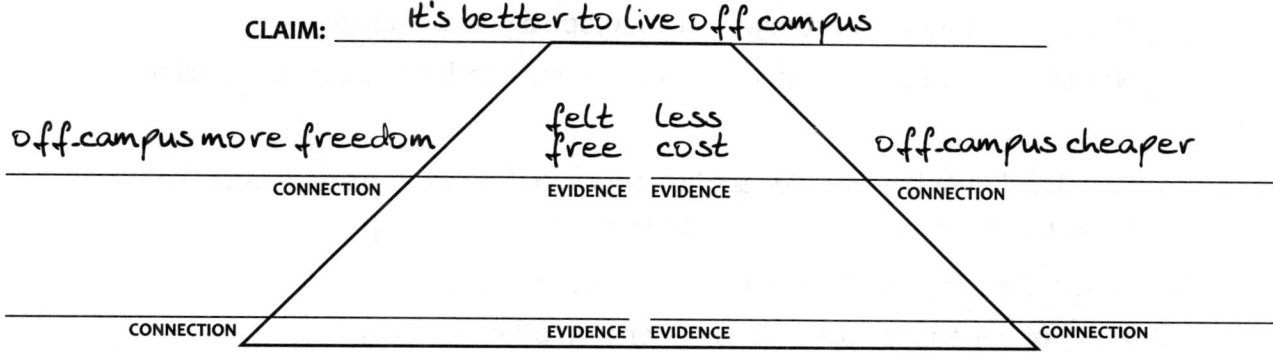

CLAIM: _It's better to live off campus_

Off-campus more freedom
CONNECTION

felt free
EVIDENCE

less cost
EVIDENCE

Off-campus cheaper
CONNECTION

CONNECTION

EVIDENCE

EVIDENCE

CONNECTION

E *Evaluate*

Evaluate the claims and evidence. Does the evidence make sense? Are you convinced?

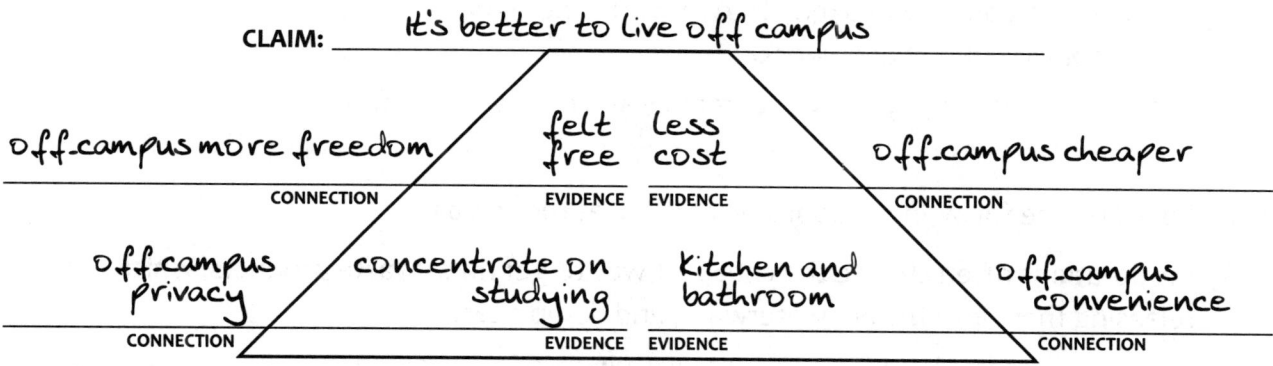

CLAIM: _It's better to live off campus_

Off-campus more freedom
CONNECTION

felt free
EVIDENCE

less cost
EVIDENCE

Off-campus cheaper
CONNECTION

Off-campus privacy
CONNECTION

concentrate on studying
EVIDENCE

Kitchen and bathroom
EVIDENCE

Off-campus convenience
CONNECTION

? **3.** In the passage, is the evidence convincing?

The evidence is reasonably convincing. However, it is only one person's experience. Maybe your sister got a great deal on rent in a nice place, or maybe prices have risen. Maybe you have different priorities and want to be near your classes, meet other students, and experience campus life. Still, there is a clear claim and relevant evidence in her letter.

Practice It!

Answer the following questions about claims and evidence.

⭐ 1. Label each sentence as either C (claim) or E (evidence).

___ Everyone should try to eat as healthily as possible.

___ A healthy diet will help you feel better and lose weight.

___ A healthy diet is linked to fewer health problems and a longer life.

⭐ 2. Label each sentence as either C (claim) or S (support).

___ Affordable day care centers often lack trained staff and adequate safety procedures.

___ It's hard for working parents to find quality, affordable day care.

___ Quality day care can cost $15,000 to $20,000 a year per child.

___ Not all parents have a relative or family friend nearby who can lend a hand.

⭐⭐ 3. The claim is followed by five pieces of evidence, but only three are relevant support. Select the three most relevant pieces of evidence.

Claim: Our company should hire three more employees.

❑ Many of our employees have experience in other markets.

❑ We are understaffed, and employees are working overtime to make it work.

❑ Our profits are growing, and if we make cuts, we will have enough in the budget for more employees.

❑ Our company is a relaxed place to work where the employees enjoy their work.

❑ With overtime pay, we waste money and overwork staff.

⭐⭐ 4. Based on the following support, what is the author's claim?

Corporations often choose the cheapest way to get rid of waste products, which means releasing them into the air, waterways, and dump sites.

In one case, a corporation dumped 43.6 million pounds of 82 chemical substances into a waterway in New York.

Corporations often get away with dumping without so much as a "slap on the wrist."

Read the passage and answer the questions that follow.

The latest proposal by the city council to tax bicycles is simply crazy. Some residents are concerned that expanding the use of bicycles in the city could threaten their own modes of transportation. This makes no sense. There is no reason why bikes, cars, busses, and pedestrians can't all coexist.

More people riding bicycles means less car traffic, fewer road repairs, and a diminished need for parking spaces. In a world of skyrocketing obesity and diabetes, bicycles promote a healthier lifestyle, which leads to fewer health care costs. In addition, the 50-plus bicycle shops in the city bring jobs and a significant amount of money into the local economy through the cycling community and tourists.

If we follow the logic of the city council, I assume an anti-walking campaign with taxes on shoes will be the next great idea from city government.

 5. Fill out the pyramid with the claim, evidence, and connections.

CLAIM: _____

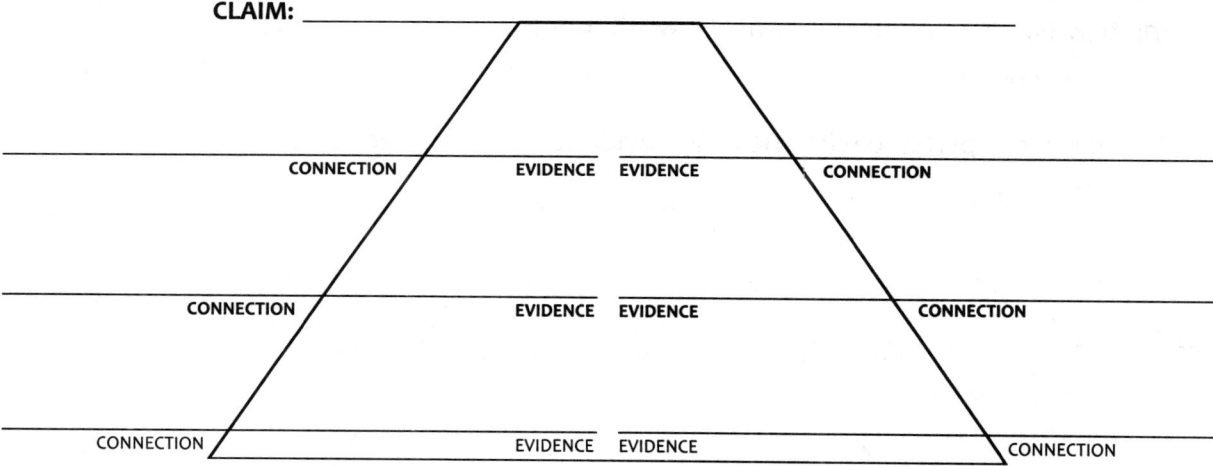

CONNECTION   EVIDENCE   EVIDENCE   CONNECTION

CONNECTION   EVIDENCE   EVIDENCE   CONNECTION

CONNECTION   EVIDENCE   EVIDENCE   CONNECTION

6. Does the evidence provide enough relevant support for the claim? Why or why not?

7. What evidence could you provide to support a tax on bicycles?

Read the passage and answer the questions that follow.

There are entirely too many overlapping layers of government in this state—particularly for those who live in metropolitan areas. The San Francisco Bay Area includes multiple city governments, several county governments, regional governments such as the Association of Bay Area Governments and the Metropolitan Transportation Commission, numerous school districts, and special districts of various kinds. Now, the governments fight with each other for taxes and attempt to shift their costs to each other.

> **Reading for Understanding**
>
> A writer often states his or her claim up front. However, sometimes you will need to infer the claim from examples and details.

The San Francisco taxpayers are taking on the burden of providing for the homeless and mentally ill from all over the region, both in and out of the city. The mayor of San Francisco refused to pay for a mental health facility that he felt the county should fund before reversing his original decision and deciding to fund it. We have a jail that has stood unused for 10 years because the county cannot afford to staff it, but other jails are overcrowded. People in different counties pay different property taxes, despite owning similar houses. Different qualities of education are available to children who live in adjoining towns. We need to learn how to work together toward a solution.

 8. Complete the pyramid with the claim, evidence, and connections.

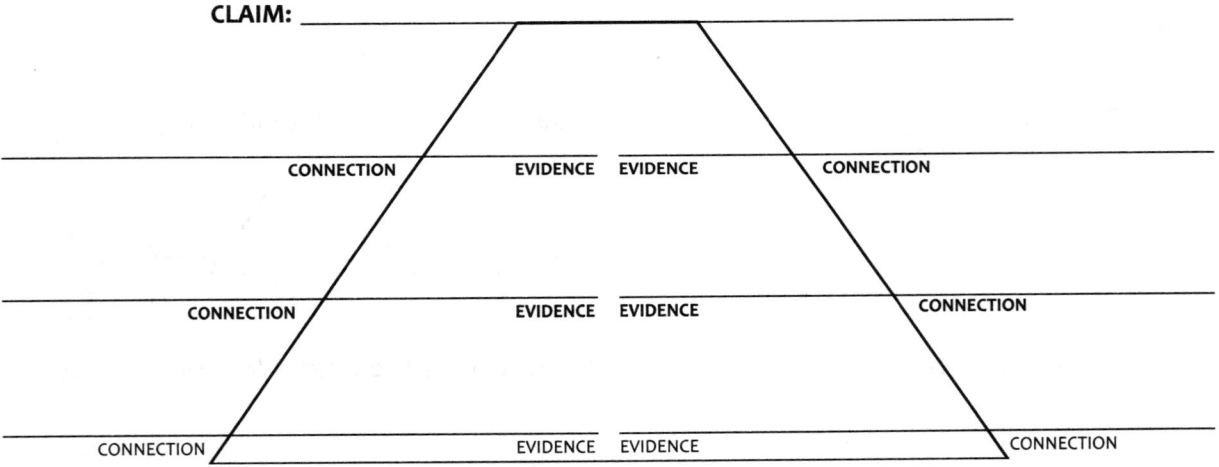

CLAIM: _____

CONNECTION   EVIDENCE   EVIDENCE   CONNECTION

CONNECTION   EVIDENCE   EVIDENCE   CONNECTION

CONNECTION   EVIDENCE   EVIDENCE   CONNECTION

9. Does the evidence provide enough relevant support for the claim? Why or why not?

Check Your Skills

Read the passage and answer the questions that follow.

This passage is from a **primary source**—a text written during a historical period being studied.

Not to Humiliate but to Win Over

Another thing that we had to get over was the fact that the nonviolent resister does not seek to humiliate or defeat the opponent but to win his friendship and understanding. This was always a cry that we had to set before people that our aim is not to defeat the white community, not to humiliate the white community, but to win the friendship of all of the persons who had perpetrated this system in the past. The end of violence or the aftermath of violence is bitterness. The aftermath of nonviolence is reconciliation and the creation of a beloved community. A boy-cott is never an end within itself. It is merely a means to awaken a sense of shame within the oppressor but the end is reconciliation, the end is redemption.

Then we had to make it clear also that the nonviolent resister seeks to attack the evil system rather than individuals who happen to be caught up in the system. And this is why I say from time to time that the struggle in the South is not so much the tension between white people and Negro people. The struggle is rather between justice and injustice, between the forces of light and the forces of darkness. And if there is a victory it will not be a victory merely for fifty thousand Negroes. But it will be a victory for justice, a victory for good will, a victory for democracy.

Another basic thing we had to get over is that nonviolent resistance is also an internal matter. It not only avoids external violence or external physical violence but also internal violence of spirit. And so at the center of our movement stood the philosophy of love. The attitude that the only way to ultimately change humanity and make for the society that we all long for is to keep love at the center of our lives. Now people used to ask me from the beginning what do you mean by love and how is it that you can tell us to love those persons who seek to defeat us and those persons who stand against us; how can you love such persons? And I had to make it clear all along that love in its highest sense is not a sentimental sort of thing, not even an affectionate sort of thing.

Source: From "The Power of Non-violence," a speech by Martin Luther King, Jr., June 04, 1957, available at: http://teachingamericanhistory.org/library/document/the-power-of-non-violence/

1. What is King's main argument in this speech?

   a. Nonviolence defeats the opponent without humiliation and through love.

   b. Nonviolence has its benefits, but doesn't convince anyone of anything.

   c. Love is not a sentimental thing, but a way to fight oppression.

   d. There is a time and a place for nonviolence, but this time is not one of them.

2. Which of the following reasons does King give to support his claim?

   a. Winning is important no matter what the cost.

   b. Violence creates bitterness.

   c. Nonviolence causes problems for protestors.

   d. Humiliating the white community is the ultimate goal.

3. King says he fights against injustice instead of fighting against white people. What is the connection between this point and the claim?

   a. It is a way to humiliate the opponent through shame.

   b. It is a violent approach that breaks down the community.

   c. It is a nonviolent approach that promotes eventual unity.

   d. It is a way to bring about eventual reversal of race roles.

4. How does King use the idea of love to support his main argument?

   a. He says non-violent protest is founded on the same principles as romantic love.

   b. He says non-violent protest is founded on a special doctrine of loving only your enemies.

   c. He says non-violent protest means to love fellow protestors through the hard times.

   d. He says non-violent protest means to love your opposition as fellow humans.

5. Give one piece of evidence to support the opposing claim that nonviolence is ineffective.

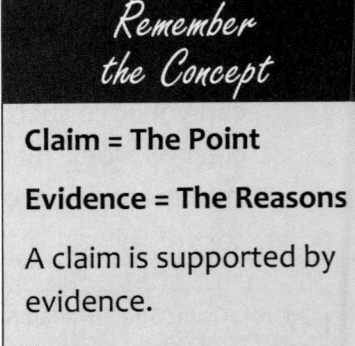

Remember the Concept

Claim = The Point

Evidence = The Reasons

A claim is supported by evidence.

Essential Writing & Language Skills

Interactive Practice Workbook

Authors

Maya Moore

Teresa Perrin

Jenni Romano

Nancy Schnog

Senior Consultants

Bonnie Goonen

Susan Pittman-Shetler

Published by Essential Education

Increase Extended Response and Essay Scores

Learn strategies for developing ideas and expressing them clearly through writing. Using the Plan, Draft, Evaluate, Submit process, students develop stronger, more persuasive writing.

Lessons are divided into four sections that connect new ideas to familiar concepts, demonstrate strategies for making writing decisions, provide guided practice that expands students' understanding, and give the opportunity to show the skill with HSE-style questions.

This 412-page book covers workplace, social studies, and science writing and develops extended response writing skills to prepare for the GED® test, TASC test, or HiSET® exam. Aligned to Common Core and College and Career Readiness Standards, this book can be used to complement a test preparation course or as a stand-alone study guide.

This writing book contains practice problems that involve several levels of knowledge and thinking.

★ If an exercise has one star, it is testing your ability to recall and use specific skills, such as grammar and language use.

★★ If an exercise has two stars, it asks you to interpret, summarize, or do other tasks that require some analysis. A two-star problem is checking to see if you have acquired a skill or concept.

★★★ If an exercise has three stars, it asks you to think strategically to answer a question or respond to a prompt. These exercises will require short or extended responses.

Plan, Draft, Evaluate

Connections

Have you ever...

- Had trouble starting a writing assignment?
- Written an important email to a supervisor or client?
- Composed a letter to your senator or representative?

Writing isn't just churning out words. To write successfully, you use a **process**. Whether you are emailing a client to describe company policies, writing a New Year's message to all your family, or composing a research paper for a college class, writing involves making many decisions. You choose your length, topic, words, and tone. All of those decisions affect your message and your reader.

Consciously following a writing process helps you make deliberate choices to write effectively. Use a four-step writing process to improve your writing.

 Plan: Examine your task. Who is the audience? What is the purpose? Research your topic, read and examine source materials, brainstorm ideas, and think through what you want to say.

 Draft: Prewrite and compose your work. You might start with a central idea, some supporting ideas, and evidence or examples. Then, fill in details, connections, transitions, and conclusions.

 Evaluate: As you work, evaluate your writing. Is it successful? Does it communicate? Continue to plan, revise, and edit your draft.

 Submit: When your work is ready, make final changes and publish. That might mean posting your work on your blog, submitting a paper to your professor, or mailing a letter to a company.

Use the first three steps together. As you **plan**, prewrite and evaluate. As you **draft**, plan and evaluate. As you **evaluate**, plan, rewrite, and edit.

Plan, Draft, and Evaluate Your Writing

The writing process helps you approach writing thoughtfully so you can improve your skills. You will make conscious decisions as you plan, draft, and evaluate.

Imagine you need to make a recommendation to your boss about which printer to purchase for the office. You work in a busy office that prints up to 1,000 pages per day. Examine the table and write a recommendation, including your reasoning.

	Price	Speed (Pages per Minute)	Monthly Workload	Ink Cost (Cents per Page)
Printer A	$459	24 ppm	70,000 pages	4.2
Printer B	$624	28 ppm	50,000 pages	2.3

Plan

First, examine your task. What is your purpose? Who is your audience? Is this a formal or informal task? What do you need to read and understand? What do you want to say? Strategies that help you think through writing tasks and plan your writing include:

- Defining purpose and audience

- Brainstorming

- Researching

Writing doesn't occur in a vacuum. Developing good ideas and strong content depends on reading and investigating as well as thinking and prewriting.

? **1.** Determine which printer to recommend. Give two reasons why.

> **Technology Tip**
>
> If you are working on a computer, keep a copy of your prewriting as you write so you don't lose your ideas.

You might recommend Printer B. Although it is more expensive, it will cost 1.9 cents less per page in ink. At 1,000 pages a day, the savings is $20 per day. Printer B is also slightly faster.

Draft

When you start writing, you won't usually just sit down and begin composing sentences. First, develop a structure or outline, and fill in some important details and ideas. Then, complete your draft. Even a short project will have a beginning, a middle, and an ending.

?   **2.** Draft a response with a beginning, middle, and ending to recommend a printer.

You might write:

> I recommend Printer B because it will be more cost effective. Printer A costs approximately $175 less than Printer B, but Printer B has an ink cost of 1.9 cents per page less than Printer A. At 1,000 pages per day, the savings in ink will be approximately $20 per day. It will take less than two weeks to recoup the extra cost of Printer B. Workload and print speed are minor factors. Both printers can handle our monthly workload (about 30,000 pages) equally well, but Printer B has a slightly faster print speed. Printer B is clearly the best choice based on the available data.

Notice that this paragraph has a beginning (stating the recommendation), a middle (giving specific evidence), and an ending (summing up the recommendation).

Evaluate

All writing can be improved. During and after writing, evaluate your work and make changes:

- **Read critically:** Approach your text with fresh eyes to improve it.
- **Revise:** Make changes to organization, tone, and content.
- **Edit:** Reorganize, improve language, and clear up confusing passages.

?   **3.** Review your paragraph. Make revisions to improve it.

You might clarify ideas, improve the organization, or add details.

Submit

                                                         Submit

When you are satisfied that your writing is ready, proofread to make any final corrections and format your work in its final form. Then publish your work—send your email or letter, submit your paper, or post your blog entry.

?   **4.** Proofread your paragraph and make any final corrections.

Make a note of common errors in your writing to help you catch mistakes when you proofread. In an office, the final step would be to send or give your recommendation to your boss.

Use your understanding of the writing process to complete the following exercises.

 1. Sharon needs to write a paper about the history of ranching in her state. How can she plan before she begins to write?

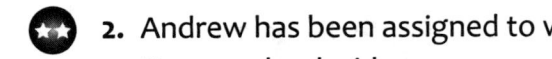 **2.** Andrew has been assigned to write an essay about the U.S. Congress for a civics class. How can he decide on a more specific topic?

3. Ralph is writing a report for work to analyze productivity in his department.

a. What does Ralph need to think about before he begins writing?

b. How can Ralph approach writing the report to keep it organized?

c. How can Ralph evaluate his writing?

 4. Mauricio intends to write about nuclear-powered submarines for a science paper. He has made a list of information he knows about submarines and has found three books about how they function.

a. Where is Mauricio in the writing process?

b. What advice would you give to Mauricio to proceed?

> *The Writing Process*
>
> 💡 **Plan**
>
> Brainstorm twice for unfamiliar topics. First, brainstorm questions about the topic. Research and then brainstorm again, including ideas and more questions.

Use the following passage for exercise 5.

Solar flares have a direct effect on the Earth's atmosphere. The intense radiation from a solar flare travels to Earth in eight minutes. As a result, the Earth's upper atmosphere becomes more ionized and expands. Long-distance radio signals can be disrupted by the resulting change in the Earth's ionosphere. A satellite's orbit around the Earth can be disturbed by the enhanced drag on the satellite from the expanded atmosphere, and satellites' electronic components can be damaged.

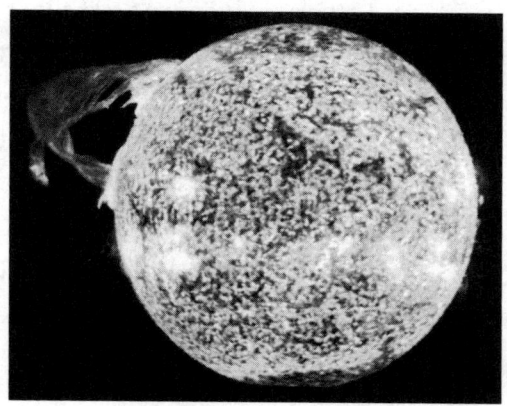

Source: Adapted from "Why Study Solar Flares?" at The Solar Flare Theory Educational Web Pages by NASA's Goddard Space Flight Center. http://hesperia.gsfc.nasa.gov/sftheory/studyflare.htm

 5. Explain possible advantages of being able to predict solar flares.

    a. 💡 **Plan:** What is the purpose and audience? What will you write?

    b. ✏️ **Draft:** Draft a paragraph to fulfill this writing task.

    c. ⚙️ **Evaluate and** ⬤ Submit ⬤ **:** Evaluate your paragraph to revise and edit it.

6. How does revising your work as you evaluate it differ from proofreading work that you are finalizing?

Use the following letter to the editor for exercise 7.

I strongly disagree with last Sunday's editorial against the city's plan to close the Bradley Branch Library. Libraries do have valuable services, but they are being replaced by services available over the Internet. Is the Bradley Library bustling with readers every day? I doubt it, otherwise the city would not choose to close it. It is natural that when people can download unlimited ebooks from the Internet and browse unlimited websites, the city should reduce its number of libraries. Patrons can travel a little further to another branch.

7. Critique the argument in this letter to the editor. Is the reasoning sound? What are possible counterarguments?

    a. **Plan:** What is the purpose and audience? What will you write?

    b. **Draft:** Draft a paragraph to fulfill this writing task.

    c. **Evaluate and** **Submit**: Evaluate your paragraph and revise it.

8. Imagine that you are planning to write a blog post to share a recipe. How would you use the writing process?

 Check **Your Skills**

Use the writing process to write short responses to the following exercises.

1. Lee is writing a blog post describing how to build a shed. He begins to draft his post. Two paragraphs later, after describing the steps, he runs out of things to say. His post seems too short, and he's not sure what to do. Describe how Lee can use the writing process to improve his writing and revise his blog post.

   Write your answer below or type your response on a computer. Take approximately 25 minutes to respond.

The Essential Writing & Language Skills workbook includes a self-evaluation tool to help students learn to critically evaluate and revise their writing.

The Writing Process

Evaluate

Don't be afraid to revise. Revision is not a failure. It is an opportunity to make good writing even better. The best writers became great writers by learning to revise—again and again.

Use the questions on page 329 to evaluate your response.

The following passage is from the book *Are Women People?* by Alice Duer Miller. The book is a collection of short passages and poetry in support of giving women the right to vote.

Use the following passage for exercise 2.

The Logic of the Law

In 1875 the Supreme Court of Wisconsin in denying the petition of women to practice before it said: "It would be shocking to man's reverence for womanhood and faith in woman ... that woman should be permitted to mix professionally in all the nastiness which finds its way into courts of justice."

It then names thirteen subjects as unfit for the attention of women—three of them are crimes committed against women.

Source: From *Are Women People?* by Alice Duer Miller, 1915.

 2. Explain and critique this passage as an argument that women should be allowed to argue cases before courts. Write your answer below or type your response on a computer. Take approximately 25 minutes to respond.

The Essential Writing & Language Skills workbook includes a self-evaluation tool to help students learn to critically evaluate and revise their writing.

Remember the Concept

Plan, Draft, Evaluate before you submit.

The Writing Process

Submit

Use the questions on page 329 to evaluate your response.

Evaluating Arguments

Connections

Have you ever...

- Watched an infomercial for a new product?

- Listened to a talk radio show about a political topic?

- Read an editorial in a newspaper or online?

Commercials, talk radio, TV shows, and editorials all present arguments. A commercial tries to convince you to buy a product. A talk show or editorial presents an opinion. How do you know who to believe or what evidence you can trust? How do you explain why one argument is more believable than another?

Arguments can be crafted to make you respond emotionally or to seem logical, even if they are not. Many arguments sound perfectly reasonable the first time you read or hear them. On further examination, you may begin to see weaknesses.

A successful argument proves its claim using relevant evidence and sound reasoning. To evaluate whether an argument is credible and sound, describe the elements of the argument:

- Is its claim clear?

- Is the evidence credible?

- Is the speaker reliable?

After you describe the claim, evidence, and speaker, use this information to write an evaluation of the argument.

Describe the Claim, Evidence, and Speaker

When you evaluate an argument, you aren't giving your own opinion of the topic. Your goal is to objectively analyze the author's argument. This skill will help you write about arguments and make decisions about controversial topics.

When you describe the claim, evidence, and speaker, you assign value. For example, if you describe a claim as unreasonable and unclear, then it is not a strong claim. If you describe evidence as specific, credible, and from a trusted source, it is strong evidence.

Examine the following argument.

Two years of college education should be available free to all qualified U.S. students. By 2018, over 60 percent of jobs will require workers with at least some college education, but public support of education is down in 48 states. At the same time, employers are cutting back (or at least not expanding) their training programs. They are, in essence, expecting candidates to show up fully qualified, according to an article in the *Las Vegas Review-Journal*.[1]

Two years of free postsecondary education would address the problem of filling jobs with qualified workers. Government investment in free higher education would stimulate the economy by allowing college graduates more spending capacity. More people would attend college if finances weren't a barrier. Other countries who make this investment see a payoff in the quality of their work forces and lifestyles.

The benefits of this policy are obvious. Students would be more motivated to graduate high school, knowing that they have options after they graduate. Under this policy, students would decide immediately on a major or training program best suited to them and would be more likely to finish quickly and begin working.

Currently, a college degree is out of reach to many students, limiting their potential. A lack of college education prevents young adults from being financially stable enough to support a family, buy a home, or start a business. Even those who graduate college aren't assured of financial security. Those who leave college owing thousands in student loans and still can't find work are in grave financial situations. A free two-year degree would help many young people get started in careers. This would benefit individuals and also the society to which they contribute.

[1] "By 2018, 60 percent of job openings will require college education," Eli Amdur, *Las Vegas Review-Journal,* available at http://www.reviewjournal.com/news/education/2018-60-percent-job-openings-will-require-college-education

Evaluating Arguments

Claim

Describe the Claim

First, identify the claim, which is the idea that the writer is attempting to prove. Summarize the claim in one sentence. Then, describe the claim. You can use the following words to describe the claim. Identify reasons for your description.

Negative ➡	Claim	⬅ Positive
Unreasonable	Somewhat reasonable	Reasonable
Unclear	Somewhat clear	Clear

? **1.** Identify and describe the claim of the argument, giving reasons for your description.

The claim is clear: that two years of college education should be free to U.S. students. It is stated at the beginning of the argument. The claim is somewhat reasonable. The government provides many services and could expand public education by two years. However, this would incur significant costs and changes in the educational system.

Describe the Evidence

Evidence

MATERIAL EVIDENCE

Use **STAR Support** criteria to examine the evidence. Is it **Specific, Timely, Accurate,** and **Relevant**? Be sure to evaluate the source. Is the source untrustworthy or unknown? Is the source an expert?

Evidence must also be **sufficient.** There must be enough evidence to prove the claim. Use the following words to describe evidence.

Negative ➡	Evidence	⬅ Positive
Insufficient/vague	Some evidence	Specific
Out-of-date	Unknown date	Timely
Inaccurate	Unknown source	Accurate
Irrelevant	Somewhat relevant	Relevant

? **2.** Describe the evidence in the argument, giving reasons for your description.

One piece of evidence that is specific, timely, accurate, and relevant is that over 60% of jobs will require degrees by 2018. This fact comes from a newspaper article. Other statements are vague, such as the idea that students would quickly decide on majors. This idea isn't supported by specifics and seems mainly to be speculation. It has no source. Overall, the evidence seems insufficient, especially since it does not address the costs of the proposal.

Speaker

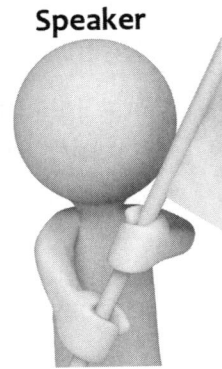

Describe the Speaker

The speaker is the author of an argument. Some speakers are biased, such as a company trying to sell a product. Others are reliable experts.

Many speakers are unknown, except through their arguments. A speaker who makes contradictory statements or uses emotional pleas to distract from the argument is not trustworthy. Also examine how the speaker addresses arguments from the opposition. Does the author ignore opponents?

Negative ➡	Speaker	⬅ Positive
Untrustworthy/biased Ignores or misrepresents opponents	Unknown Acknowledges opponents	Expert Addresses legitimate counterarguments

? **3.** Describe the speaker, giving reasons for your description.

The speaker's expertise or bias is unknown. He or she acknowledges that the opposition exists but does not address any counterarguments. The speaker is also somewhat contradictory. The statement that college graduates often cannot find jobs undermines the idea that two years of free college is a solution.

Write an Evaluation

Combine your descriptions of the claim, speaker, and evidence to write an evaluation. Start with a central idea that states the overall strength or weakness of the argument and use specific details to explain your descriptions of the claim, speaker, and evidence. Your evaluation should have a beginning, middle, and ending.

? **4.** Write a paragraph evaluating the argument.

The Essential Skills Series workbooks all include comprehensive answers and explanations to help the student learn.

See the Answers and Explanations section on page 384 for a sample response.

Use the following passage for exercises 1 through 4.

Holiday parades are a waste of public resources. They are admittedly festive and happy occasions, but they serve no civic purpose that couldn't be otherwise served by a concert, fireworks show, or fair. Marching bands can be heard at football games, and balloons and floats are simply unnecessary diversions.

At famous parades, such as the Macy's Thanksgiving Day Parade or Mardi Gras, viewers, who are often inebriated, gather in the streets only to watch other people walk at various speeds. These parades block traffic and create trash. They require police and emergency responder overtime. This cost would be better spent funding environmental programs, shelters, education, and other public services.

1. Describe the claim in the passage, giving reasons for your description.

2. Describe the evidence in the passage, giving reasons for your description.

3. Describe the speaker in the passage, giving reasons for your description.

4. Write a well-organized paragraph evaluating the argument. Include suggestions to improve the argument.

> *The Writing Process*
>
> ⚙ **Evaluate**
>
> When you evaluate your writing, describe your claim, evidence, and yourself as a speaker. Look for ways to develop your reliability as a speaker. One way is by acknowledging the opposition and respectfully responding to counterarguments.

Use the following passage for exercises 5 through 8.

Driverless cars are our future, and we should encourage their development by passing laws allowing driverless cars on roads throughout the country. Nevada, Florida, and California already have laws allowing driverless cars. These software-controlled cars have successfully navigated San Francisco's steep and twisting Lombard Street and driven over 300,000 miles of tests. Only one accident has happened during testing: a human driver rear-ended a driverless car. With their incredible record of safety, driverless cars will reduce drunk driving, make commutes more productive, and reduce insurance costs. In a March 2012 video posted by Google, a legally blind man goes through a drive-through in a self-driving Toyota Prius. This video highlights the benefits of driverless car technology to disabled people. Why not allow this safe and beneficial technology to flourish?

5. Describe the claim in the passage, giving reasons for your description.

6. Describe the evidence in the passage, giving reasons for your description.

7. Describe the speaker in the passage, giving reasons for your description.

8. Write a well-organized paragraph evaluating the argument. Include suggestions to improve the argument.

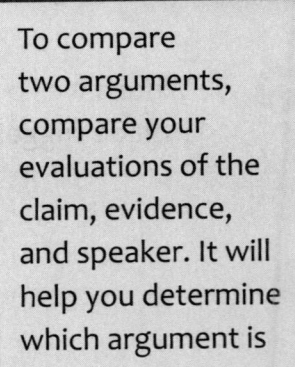

Build Your Writing Skills

To compare two arguments, compare your evaluations of the claim, evidence, and speaker. It will help you determine which argument is stronger and why.

Check Your Skills

Use the following passages for exercise 1.

The presence of royalty gives a nation a sense of pride and history that should be cherished and honored. Great Britain is an excellent example of what a royal family can add to the culture. The constitutional monarchy allows Britain to experience the best of both worlds: the continuity of tradition and the progressive possibilities of a democracy.

Around the world, people celebrate royal weddings and births. When Prince Charles and Lady Diana married, it was an international sensation. An estimated 750 million people watched. The birth of Prince George of Cambridge in 2013 spurred composer Paul Mealor to write a new lullaby, "Sleep On." Shared events like this bring a nation together, forming cultural milestones.

In Great Britain and other nations with historic monarchies, the royal family is a link to the past. Although royal roles may be ceremonial, a royal family allows the average citizen to celebrate a shared history and national pride.

The family of the Prince of Wales: Engraving by Shyubler. Published in the magazine *Niva*, published by A.F. Marx, St. Petersburg, Russia, 1888

Royalty devalues the average citizen. A monarchy flies in the face of the idea that "all men are created equal." If royalty were eliminated, any loss of tradition would be more than replaced by a thirst for innovation, improvement, and individuality.

Through its monarchy, Great Britain makes a silent statement that some people are inherently better than others. Members of the royal family have special treatment because of an accident of birth. In an article on CNN, Graham Smith details the problems with British monarchy. He states, "It is secretive, having recently lobbied successfully to have itself removed entirely from the reaches of our Freedom of Information laws; it lobbies government ministers for improvements to its financial benefits and for its own private agenda; it is hugely costly—an estimated £202 million a year."[1] The British monarchy is outdated, undemocratic, and costly. On the other hand, the U.S. system of democracy, where anyone might earn the presidency, encourages self-improvement because birth is not destiny.

---

[1]Source: "Why UK should abolish its 'failed' monarchy" by Graham Smith on CNN.com
http://www.cnn.com/2012/05/30/world/europe/uk-jubilee-republicans/index.html

1. Analyze the two arguments to determine which position is best supported. Use relevant and specific evidence from both passages to support your response.

   Write your answer below or type your response on a computer. Take approximately 45 minutes to respond.

The Essential Writing & Language Skills workbook includes a self-evaluation tool to help students learn to critically evaluate and revise their writing.

Remember the Concept

Describe the **claim, evidence,** and **speaker** to evaluate an argument.

Use the questions on page 329 to evaluate your response.